The Data Dictionary: Concepts and Uses

The Data Dictionary: Concepts and Uses

Charles J. Wertz

QED Information Sciences, Inc.
Wellesley, Massachusetts

© 1986 by QED ® Information Sciences, Inc.
QED Plaza • P.O. Box 181
Wellesley, MA 02181

Library of Congress Catalog Card Number 86-060755
International Standard Book Number 0-89435-180-X

Printed in the United States of America.

CONTENTS

ILLUSTRATIONS

PREFACE

This book is based on a combination of practical experience and theory. The specific topic is the implementation of a data dictionary. It is nearly impossible to separate this from the use of data base management systems, data administration concepts, and notions about information and its uses in organizations. The book is intended for a broad audience. I hope the reader with a lot of background in computer systems and programming will bear with me when I take time out to explain some of the more basic concepts. I'd like to suggest that you read these sections even if they seem very familiar. A common understanding of each topic is important to the overall development of the book.

If the book helps you to understand the issues involved in installing a data dictionary; or, better yet, if it helps you succeed in such a task, I will have met my primary objective.

This book is not a technical reference to the inner workings of any specific data dictionary software product. It is not a substitute for careful reading of the technical manuals provided by the vendors. It is a complement to this technical documentation. It discusses concepts and problems that are frequently ignored or dealt with summarily in technical documents. There are two main reasons for this approach. First, specific technical details can vary considerably from one data dictionary to another, even though the same basic concepts underlie each. It is very easy to get lost in the specific details of one product. It is important to see beyond these details to the basic concepts. If I can help you to do this, we will have made great progress toward the primary objective.

The second reason for my approach to this book is that the vendors of data dictionaries are constantly improving and updating their products. It is in the nature of our business that by the time a book such as this is written, edited, and published, enhancements to the products discussed will have been developed. As a general rule, the basic concepts will not have been altered, but many details and interfaces will have been. Thus, there is no point in pretending that a book like this can take the place of the vendors' manuals and training programs. It can, and will, provide a background that will make the details more meaningful to you.

The book is not a cookbook. There are too many possible variations in organizations and objectives and problems. You should, however, be able to use this material to create a plan and a dictionary uniquely suited to your particular needs. Some of the material is more theoretical than that which you might find in a vendor's technical manual, but I've tried to keep it as practical and down-to-earth as possible.

I've attempted to bring together material and issues that are not dealt with by other books on data dictionaries and data administration. I view this book as complementary to many of the cited references. I recommend that you read some of them, as well.

The sequence of material more or less follows my own ''pilgrim's progress'' into the world of data dictionaries and data administration. Thus, there is some circularity and repetition. This is intentional. I believe that if you'll bear with me you will gain a thorough comprehension of the subject.

Chapter 1 reviews some basic data concepts and data-related problems. The problems provide our motive for developing a data dictionary. I'd be surprised if you weren't already familiar with many of these.

Chapter 2 discusses various approaches to the solution of these problems. You should understand that there is a relationship between each of these and the data dictionary. Again, you are likely to be familiar with many of these topics.

Chapter 3 is a discussion of the concepts and features of data dictionaries. You will see that the first big problem is deciding what the term *data dictionary* really means.

Chapters 4, 5, and 6 review three specific products: Cullinet's Integrated Data Dictionary, IBM's DB/DC Data Dictionary, and Manager Products' DATAMANAGER. These chapters show how the concepts discussed in Chapter 3 are embodied in actual software.

Chapter 7 describes a simple but fairly typical dictionary design. The purpose is to clarify concepts. It is not intended to tell you exactly how your dictionary should look. The sequence of this chapter reflects the sequence in which you might encounter the various issues if you were a naive user of a data dictionary.

Chapter 8 introduces several new problems. Many people encounter these after they are well into the process of installing a dictionary. The idea is, of course, that you will be better off if you address these issues before you get in too deep.

Chapter 9 relates the material covered in the preceding chapters to the problems and possible solutions discussed in Chapters 1 and 2. Chapter 10 offers ideas for much broader use of a dictionary.

Chapter 11 provides a step-by-step checklist for planning the implementation of a data dictionary. You might wish I had been more specific and tried to tell you exactly what to do, but I don't think it is possible to do this in a generic way. There are too many differences in organizations and approaches to data processing. I do provide steps to follow and questions to ask. I also offer specific suggestions whenever I feel I can do that.

Chapter 12 offers a few parting remarks.

1 Basic Data Concepts and Problems

1.1 THE VALUE OF INFORMATION

This book emphasizes the use of a data dictionary, but the real topic is management of data and conversion of data into information. The data dictionary, as we shall see, is a tool that facilitates these activities. Overemphasis of the tool can be like expecting the tail to wag the dog. Management, control, and operation of any organization involve the transmission, processing, and storage of information. If that information is timely, consistent, accurate, understandable—and, above all, usable—it is a valuable resource. Effective use of a data dictionary can help in the management of this resource. Misdirected or ineffective use of a data dictionary is not only no help, it is likely to be a hindrance.

1.2 DATA VERSUS INFORMATION

Understanding the distinction between data and information is essential. Data can be just about any string of numbers or letters, arranged in any way. In data processing, we tend to use the word *data* to mean anything recorded in machine-readable form, whether or not it is factual data. We also tend to use the word *information* to mean the result of organizing the data in some meaningful or useful way.

Computerized data processing is a relatively new human activity. It has existed for thirty or forty years, at most. An explosion of technology, ideas, and terminology has occurred—and it is still going on. These innovations have not come about through an orderly evolution. One result is that we must be careful about words—data and information, for example. Many of the terms used in this book mean very different things to different people, so we will try to define each important term carefully.

It is, however, very difficult to define precisely words like data, facts, and information. For our purposes, it is best to think of data as a raw material and information as something that can be produced or derived from that raw material.[1] Information provides the basis for operation, control, and management of a business or enterprise.[2]

The process of managing any enterprise involves, among other things, gathering, organizing, and using relevant data. *Using* is a key word here. If it can't be located and used, the data or information has no value. People who are concerned with managing businesses, governments, and other organizations are becoming more aware of the value of accurate information and the cost incurred when accurate information cannot be obtained. We are going to be looking at some of the things that can be done to provide high-quality information.

1.3 THE INFORMATION TRIANGLE

It is convenient to divide information and information-processing activities into three categories that reflect operating, controlling and planning functions. This concept is usually represented by a triangle like the one shown in Figure 1.1.

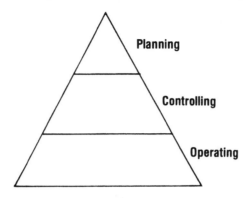

FIGURE 1.1 The Information Triangle

In the context of our discussion, the term *operating* refers to the day-to-day activities of an organization and the detailed data that supports or is generated by these activities. Most decision making at this level proceeds according to well-defined rules. Examples include subtracting the amount of a check from a bank balance, calculating a customer's bill at a supermarket, or assembling automobiles. Such activities and the supporting data or information form the base of the information triangle.

The word *controlling* refers to activities that involve aggregation and decision making. The data or information used is usually obtained by summarizing or interpreting the operating data. Often the decision making is based on relatively well-defined rules, as in operating activities. If a bank has too many delinquent loans, credit policy may be made more restrictive. If a wholesaler raises prices, the supermarket may increase retail prices. If an automobile manufacturer starts running low on some part, more will be ordered. However, the rules for controlling activities often are not as rigid or well-defined as those applying to operating activities.

The peak of the triangle represents *planning*. Obtaining the required information usually involves gathering, merging, and interpreting. In addition, these activities require a great deal of judgement, but there are fewer rules in planning. Should the bank open a branch near a large new subdivision? Should the supermarket stock auto parts? Should the auto maker diversify by buying a data processing company? These decisions are often based on intuition. (This last statement bothers many people, but it is true.) The high-level manager must find patterns in large amounts of data. It is often necessary for a manager to create abstractions and to rely on ''feel'' to do this.

1.4 TRADITIONAL INFORMATION SYSTEMS

How do all the foregoing observations relate to the short history of computers and data processing? Most organizations incorporated computers into their operations by implementing computer programs and systems for one business activity at a time. The applications selected were easy to define, involved repetition and rules, appeared to result in cost savings by replacing human labor, and were politically acceptable.[3] Payroll, general accounting, bank deposit accounting, and inventory are common examples. In each case, the job of putting the application on the computer involved obtaining a definition of the pertinent rules from someone, designing input and output forms, writing the programs, and installing the system.

Generally, these implementations did not significantly alter the way an enterprise did things—at least not at the outset. The routine, repetitive tasks were automated; they were not redefined or changed. The major benefit was usually the ability to manipulate much more data in a given period of time.

Even though the tasks given over to the computer proceeded according to fixed rules, many bad and even unusable systems were developed. Usually the cause was failure to gain an adequate understanding of the procedures *and the data* involved before writing the programs.

An individual programmer or a team of analysts and programmers normally develop a system by working with the people in the specific segment of the enterprise that will be affected: the payroll department or accounts receivable, for example. Consequently, the view of the enterprise held by the payroll department forms the basis for the payroll system, while the view held by the manager of accounts receivable permeates the accounts receivable system. Often these views are surprisingly limited and inconsistent. This is an important point: *new business systems are based on an organization's view of itself.* This view is not imposed by technology. Only after a system has been in use for a while does it become part of the infrastructure and have an impact on the organization's self-image. That, however, is a different issue.

As the use of computer systems increases within a given enterprise, several trends are usually evident.

More of the controls and rudimentary decision making processes are incorporated into the programs. Inventory systems begin to generate purchase orders automatically. Credit card systems begin to authorize or refuse to authorize the extension of credit without human intervention.

There is a growing realization that data and processing relationships exist among diverse systems, and an effort is made to take advantage of them.[4]

Managers become interested in the possibility that data and information processing can be used to help the enterprise gain a competitive advantage in the marketplace.[5]

Managers become aware of problems that can be caused by misused or poorly understood data.[6]

Managers and data processing technicians become aware of problems that occur when information system designs are not based on a thorough understanding of the organization's structure, goals, and plans.[7]

We'll be taking a much closer look at these issues in the next section of this chapter. For the moment, just note that controlling forms the next level of the triangle, that it becomes necessary to gather or summarize information or data from the operational systems, and that *this can be done only if the design of the operational systems allows it.* Frequently these higher level systems do change the way the enterprise conducts its activities—*they will work well only if things change.*

1.5 PROBLEMS

The preceding discussion has been extremely general, and you may already have been familiar with much of the material. Now we are going to review some of the problems.

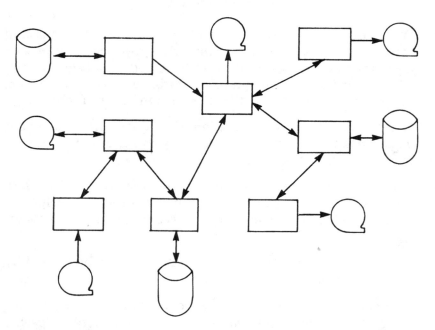

FIGURE 1.2 Typical Network of Programs and Files

Take a look at Figure 1.2. This diagram illustrates a typical collection of computer programs and systems as they exist in many organizations today. The rectangles represent systems. The stylized pictures of tapes and disks represent data files.

The lines relate files to systems. Since the same data is relevant to activities of several different systems, it is necessary to maintain multiple records of the same data and to pass copies back and forth. This is so because individual systems are usually built to serve different aspects of a business but those different aspects are not entirely unrelated. Figure 1.3 shows that the base of the information triangle consists of these independently conceived processing systems, with their unique data files. The next levels of the triangle represent information generated by exchanges of information between these systems, and, in a few rare cases, by sharing the same data files.

Do you think there might be a better way to share information? If you do, you are not alone. We are going to discuss several problems associated with this kind of information architecture.[8] It is easy to subdivide these problems into two categories: operating problems and data-related problems.

1.5.1 Operating Problems

We'll review the operating problems first. These are summarized in Figure 1.4.

Redundant Data. Frequently, the same data is maintained in multiple locations. Records of quantities of parts on order are in the inventory file and also in the purchase order file. Customer names and addresses are in the checking account file, the savings account file, the credit card file, and several other places. Costs are multiplied by storing the same information in several different files. These costs include the cost of storage space for extra copies of the data.

Redundant Processing. Costs are also multiplied by processing the same data over and over. The costs include the computer time and the human labor required to enter the same data into multiple computer systems. The increased cost of programming repetitive data description and entry routines is less obvious, but probably much more significant.

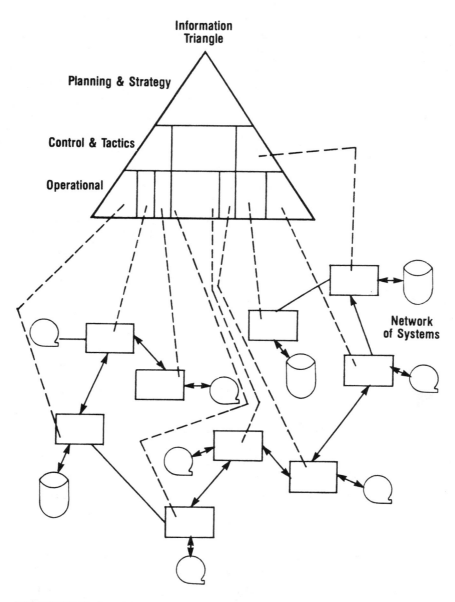

**FIGURE 1.3   The Network of Systems Forms the Base
of the Triangle**

Redundancy

Inconsistency

Complexity and Interdependence

Difficulty of Change

Lack of Documentation

FIGURE 1.4 Typical Operating Problems

Consistency and inconsistency are discussed in some detail in section 1.5. Right now, let's just note that systems need programs, routines, and procedures to verify and ensure consistency among multiple copies of the same data. Developing and operating them involves costs.

Complexity and Interdependence. In any complex network of programs and files the processing of one program or system is highly dependent on others. As complexity increases, delays and errors are propagated and proliferated. For example, an inventory system might encounter a magnetic tape read error, causing a delay in the processing of the purchasing system, which then might cause a delay in the processing of the accounts payable system, which in turn might cause a delay in the processing of the general accounting system. This sort of thing can be a serious problem for operations managers, computer programmers, and even end users.[9] Many organizations are struggling to solve such problems.

Difficulty of Change. We live in an age of change. Businesses and procedures are always changing. When a business procedure changes, the associated computer programs and systems must also change. A result of the complexity we've noted is that it can be exceedingly difficult to make changes. An apparently innocent change made to the inventory system may have a surprising effect on the operation of the general accounting system.

Understanding the seriousness of this problem is difficult if you haven't had personal experience with it. A lot of time has to be spent deciding what must or can be changed when a particular result is desired. This adds considerable cost to most development projects. It makes them much more difficult than they might otherwise be. Many executives, particularly those who manage service organizations such as banks, live in fear of the day when the complexity of the existing systems may make it impossible to react to competition and the needs of the marketplace.

Lack of Adequate Documentation. The systems architectures that have evolved are not only complex, difficult to operate, and difficult to understand; they are often very poorly documented. Skilled computer technicians always have been in short supply. Management always has seemed to be more interested in immediate results than in future problems. Most people would rather move on to new things than sit around writing explanations of old things. Consequently, they often do not develop adequate documentation for systems that would be very hard to understand even with good documentation. This problem is discussed further in section 1.5.2.

Is That All? A list like this one can be found in almost any book or paper that discusses problems with traditional systems architecture. These are real day-to-day operating problems, with measurable costs that could be reduced by adopting a different approach to data processing. However, there is another set of problems with costs that are less obvious, more difficult to quantify, and probably much greater.

1.5.2. Information-Related Problems

Let's call the second category information-related problems. These relate to the quality and availability of information. They are summarized in Figure 1.5.

Inconsistent Data
Inconsistent Representations
Inconsistent Timing
Lack of Understanding
Lack of Good Data
Lack of Organization

FIGURE 1.5   Typical Information Problems

Inconsistent Data. Philosophers and scientists like to talk about entropy or disorder in the universe. There definitely seems to be a sort of entropy in data processes. Whenever multiple files of the same information exist, it is highly likely that none of the files will match. For example, if there are multiple files of customer data, it is very likely that not all of them will contain the most current customer address or even the same spelling of the customer's name. A purchasing file might contain data indicating that 100 of a particular item are on order, while the inventory file indicates that 125 are on order.

Part of the problem can be attributed to user errors. Given several copies of a customer name and address file, there is a good chance that someone will forget to change one of them when a customer moves. Part can be attributed to errors committed by computer programmers and operators. Two different programs may process the same data differently. Data that should be transferred from one system or program to another may be overlooked.

We've already noted that operating costs are increased by repetitive processing of the same data and by the labor involved in trying to eliminate inconsistencies in that data. What about the costs incurred when discrepancies are not discovered? How many customers have been angered by errors in their records? How many incorrect decisions have been based on poor information? Can the costs associated with such problems even be estimated? The uncontrolled proliferation of personal computers compounds this problem.

Once in a great while a hardware error results in lost or inconsistent data. However, even in this case, human failure is involved. Either the overall system did not contain a procedure to detect and correct the hardware failure or someone did not correctly follow such a procedure.

Inconsistent Representations and Codes. Problems caused by inconsistent representations and codes are more subtle than the information-related problems we have just discussed. They are potentially much more costly, as well. Inconsistencies are often "designed in" in one of several possible ways. For example, it is customary to employ various coding schemes in computer systems. We might use the Standard Industrial Classification code to identify a customer's primary business. Or we might use a code to identify the customer's credit rating. If two different systems use different and inconsistent coding schemes for the same information, it may be impossible to merge data from the two systems or even to develop procedures for verifying consistency. To use another type of example, we often find that two different systems use mutually inconsistent identifiers for the same thing. For example, the purchasing file might use a purchase order number to identify a record, while the receiving file uses the vendor's shipping number.[10]

Sometimes the systems actually have inconsistent ways of looking at things built into them. An inventory system differentiates between the quantity of a given item stored in one location and the quantity stored in another. A quality control or shop scheduling system differentiates between the units in one batch or manufacturing lot and those in another. If we use the inventory system, we may be unable to determine which warehouses contain batches that may have defective units. *These types of problems frequently arise from the way an enterprise operates or is organized. The computer systems merely magnify the effect of existing problems.*

Inconsistent Timing. Different data files may be updated according to different schedules. Suppose we reconcile our inventory as of January 29 against our sales for the period ending January 30. The result will probably look fine, but what will the numbers mean?

Lack of Understanding. When we attempt to merge information from different systems or files of data bases, the result is often poor. Sometimes it is not possible to combine the information. Sometimes it is technically possible, but we have accomplished the merging by doing something analogous to adding apples (measured in bushels) and automobiles (measured in kilograms) together to produce a number. And people really use numbers developed in this manner to make decisions or prove their points!

We noted in the section on operating problems that there are costs associated with poor documentation and that inadequate documentation is common. The right kind of documentation could also eliminate, or at least mitigate, the types of problems we've been discussing here. Documentation that will resolve such problems, however, is rare indeed.

In large corporations, interactions among groups are difficult to understand. Interaction and management are difficult because of conflicting goals. Individuals lose sight of the overall organization and its purposes. In a smaller enterprise, it is more likely that individuals will have a good understanding of the overall operation. Thus, it is less likely that these information-related problems will occur, or at least less likely that they will occur without people being aware of them. On the other hand, it is less likely that a small enterprise will have formal rules and procedures and also less likely that the small operation will develop good documentation. When that small operation grows quickly, watch out!

Lack of Good Data: Out-and-Out Inaccuracies. The best technical system design in the world won't help you if no one provides good data. If the system provides for a customer credit rating code but no one puts the data in, the credit reports won't be very valuable. It is even more insidious if data are entered but not entered correctly, or if data are not kept up to date. When this happens the report or analysis looks fine, but it is completely wrong! And, a lot of people will call this a computer error instead of a human error.

This problem can stem from a poor design of the overall system that relates manual procedures to computerized operations. It can be the result of failure to document procedures or train the staff in the use of the system. It is amazing how often we install a system that cost hundreds of thousands of dollars to develop and then neglect to tell people how to use it. Sometimes we do an adequate job of training when we install a system but fail to provide adequate training for people hired after the system is in place. The problem can also stem from outright failure on the part of staff to follow procedures and from unwillingness or inability on the part of management to encourage or enforce compliance. It can occur because the staff is poorly motivated or because people already have too much to do. It may be a correctable problem or it may be a basic flaw in the system design. We often have unrealistic expectations built into our data input formats and procedures.

Lack of Organization: Even If It's There, Can You Find It? The final problem we'll address here occurs when the data is present, is consistent, and is accurate but can't be used because no one understands what is actually contained in the various files and data bases well enough to make effective use of it. This may be the saddest case of all.

1.6 Summary and Transition

Figures 1.4 and 1.5 summarize the possibilities we've just discussed. You may ask how this sort of thing can happen. It's really very common. And the explanation is simple. We've already noted that a systems analyst or project team usually develops a system on the basis of discussion with one user or user group. That user's view of things tends to be built into the programs and data files.[11]

This chapter could discuss each of these problems in much greater detail, but, it's time to summarize and move on. Data has been described as the raw material from which we construct or manufacture information. Today, many organizations are data-rich and information-poor. In some cases the problem is compounded by the presence of incorrect or incomplete data. Both operating costs and opportunity costs arise from these problems. Some costs are more difficult to isolate and quantify than others, but they are still present.

A simple example might be useful here. Suppose you would like to develop a statement of your net worth. The first thing you would look at is your bank statement or statements. If you have more than one bank account, you must gather together all the statements. It is quite possible that each set of bank statements will be in a different format. It is also possible that you may have to adjust for deposits or withdrawals or interest payments that have occurred since the statements were prepared. You may even have to call the bank(s) to obtain current information. Here's another wrinkle. If any of these are term accounts, there may be a penalty for premature withdrawal. If the purpose of drawing up your statement of net worth is to determine how much cash you can raise right now, you'll need to adjust for that.

Do you also have an account with a credit union? That must also be researched. Do you own stocks and bonds? The last statement you received from your broker will not reflect the current value of your holdings. Aside from the fact that there may have been transactions since the statement was prepared, you'll have to check today's financial pages for accurate values.

Do you have any sort of individual retirement account? Is that statement up to date? If the account contains an investment in stocks or bonds, you'll need to check the financial pages again. You probably can't actually get your hands on that amount of money. There will most likely be either a tax or interest penalty for premature withdrawal. Or perhaps you should use some elaborate formula to adjust for the time value of money.

How about the cash value of your insurance policies? The policy may contain a chart which makes it possible to calculate this value, or it may be necessary to obtain it from the insurance company. If the policy accumulates dividends it will be necessary to obtain this information from the insurance company as well.

What about the values of other types of assets? Would you go so far as to have your house appraised? An automobile dealer or banker could show you a book listing current average values for automobiles. Other assets, such as jewelry or camera equipment, might be harder to evaluate.

Of course, you'd need to calculate liabilities as well as assets. Do you know the current close-out values for any loans you may have? More than likely you'd need to ask the lenders for these.

This could go on, but we have sufficiently illustrated the point. Attempting to obtain and merge information from a variety of sources is a problem that managers of enterprises face daily. As you can see, the problems begin with deciding where to look, not with how to get and interpret the information. *It's important to note that many of these problems exist whether or not there are computer systems. Computer systems magnify these problems because they embody rigid data formats and fixed rules.*

In the next chapter, we'll survey a number of solutions that have been proposed. Then, in the remainder of the book we'll take a detailed look at the potential of one of them, the data dictionary. We'll also develop techniques for effective use of a data dictionary.

NOTES

1. The 1978 paperback edition by Ballantine Books of the *Random House Dictionary* defines data as "facts or information collected for analysis or computation" and information as "knowledge communicated or received," "knowledge gained," or "data that can be coded for processing by a computer." Common usage in data processing is based on the notion that data is a sort of raw material while information is the result of

manipulating or analyzing the data. See, for example, Raymond McLeod, Jr., *Management Information Systems* (Chicago: Science Research Associates, Inc., 1983), ch 1.

2. The word *enterprise* is often used in place of *business* to avoid limiting the discussion to a business company. Governments, schools, clubs, private individuals (including criminals) use computers and data processing to operate, control and manage their activities. See "Mob Flexing Computer Muscle to Streamline Operations," in *Computerworld*, 23 July, 1984. We will frequently use the words enterprise and organization in order to achieve this generality.

3. People with a data processing orientation use the word *application* to mean a specific use of the computer. For example, when computer technology is applied to payroll processing, the result is often called a payroll application. *Input* is data that has been translated from human-readable form to a form that allows the computer to process it. *Output* is the result of the converse process. We usually refer to a collection of computer programs and manual procedures that have been designed to automate a particular application as a *system*.

4. For example, see "The Banks' Great Struggle to Master a Tangle of Data," *Business Week* 10 December 1984.

5. See E. Warren McFarlan, "Information Technology Changes the Way You Compete," *Harvard Business Review* May–June 1984; Charles Wiseman, "Strategic Vision," *Computerworld*, 20 May 1985; Blake Ives and Gerard P. Learmonth, "The Information System as a Competitive Weapon," *Communications of the ACM* 27(December 1984). Also see *Senior Management Control of Computer Based Systems*, a set of tutorial notes by Dennis G. Severance. They were published by The Institute of Electrical and Electronics Engineers in May 1984.

6. See "How Personal Computers Can Trip Up Executives," *Business Week*, 24 September 1984.

7. See *Information Systems Planning to Meet Business Objectives: A Survey of Practices, 1983* (New York: Cresap, McCormick and Paget, Inc., 1983).

8. The use of the word *architecture* is discussed in some detail in the next chapter. See section 2.8.1.

9. It's a common practice to refer to the non-data-processing people who make use of data processing systems as *users*. This term has an unpleasant sound, but it is so common that we have to employ it. Some writers and practitioners are starting to use the word *client* instead. This sounds better as long as you don't think about the fact that social workers often refer to welfare recipients as clients.

10. Could we ask our vendors to use our purchase order numbers for shipping numbers? Some of them would do it willingly. Some would tell us that they just can't do this *because of the computer.*

11. In many organizations, especially large organizations, the data processing staff are the only ones who are really aware of the different ways different people have of viewing the enterprise and its data. Usually, they do not have sufficient influence to effect the organizational changes that would be required to solve the problems.

2   Some Possible Solutions

The preceding chapter summarized some data-related and information-related problems. This is not the first time these have been documented. In fact, it is probably obligatory for any current book on the subject of information processing to contain such a chapter. This means that the problems are widespread and well known. It also means that many attempts have been made to solve them.

This chapter contains a review of some solutions that have been suggested, along with brief comments on their success or failure, their strengths and weaknesses. Chapter 9 reviews them again and relates the use of a data dictionary to each.

2.1   DATA BASE

A theme that runs through many of the proposed solutions is that of the *data base*. This term has been used so often in so many ways that it is difficult to attach any real meaning to it. The author once participated in a GUIDE committee whose task was to prepare a paper about the application of data administration in today's environment.[1] We spent several days developing a definition of *data base.* Here's what we came up with:

> A data base is a logically organized and structured collection of interrelated data stored together without unnecessary redundancy to serve multiple applications and diverse and changing information requirements.

That's a mouthful! We won't belabor it here, but every word of the definition is important:

- Logical organization is an essential quality of a usable data base.

- A structure that embodies the data interrelationships is equally essential.

- Elimination of *unnecessary* redundancy is another key element.

- Ability to change is also critical.

Here is another approach. It is intended to be humorous, but it does capture the notion that many people have of a data base.

> A data base contains everything everyone wants to know. It is organized so that anyone can find any piece of information whenever it is needed.

A more realistic and useful definition follows. This is a paraphrase of a definition that James Martin has used in a number of his books and presentations.

A data base is a well-organized, useful collection of information. You not only have the data, you also know you have it, and you can find it when you need it.

None of these is a rigorous definition. However, taken together they convey the idea that people often have in mind when they propose a data base as the solution to data and information problems: a pool of information that can be shared by many users and business processes. This sharing is envisioned as a way to eliminate the redundancies, synchronization problems, and other difficulties that we discussed in Chapter 1.

Constructing a single, gigantic data base containing all the information used by a large enterprise such as a major corporation is no simple task. In many situations it may not even be possible! The design process requires development of an underlying data structure from which the various views required by various individuals can be derived. This is an extremely difficult and time-consuming task. *Development of such a design involves the resolution of many political problems as well as many technical problems. The political and organizational problems are usually much more formidable than the technical ones.*

The technical aspects of operating, controlling, and maintaining a large, shared data base are also significant, however. If the data is actually linked together, it becomes a prime example of the "all the eggs in one basket" approach. Recovery from a serious hardware or software error will be exceedingly difficult and time consuming. Coordinating and controlling the processing of all updates and inquiries that interact with an integrated data base can be a major operational problem.

For most large organizations, a single, integrated data base is a dream that is not susceptible to realization. On the other hand, implementation of a relatively small number of well-designed data bases would probably provide most large enterprises with much better information and information-processing capabilities than they possess today.[2] This is not intended as a condemnation of the data base concept. Rather, it is intended to indicate that the implementation of sound and useful data bases is a difficult and time-consuming process that must be approached with caution.

2.1.1 A Different Sort of Data Base

We'd better pause to take note of another common use of the term *data base*. Many commercial services provide access to banks of data such as stock and bond prices, airline schedules, the text of an encyclopedia, current news bulletins, and so on. Our definition of data base doesn't exclude these but we should be aware that they are very specialized. We usually are not thinking of such data bases when we use the term data base in this book.

2.2 DATA BASE MANAGEMENT SYSTEMS

A data base management system (DBMS) is a software tool that provides facilities for the management of data and of data bases, large or small. Today, it is necessary to differentiate between a DBMS designed for a large mainframe environment and one designed for a micro or personal computer environment. This is true even though some of the personal computers are getting to be anything but micro.

Figure 2.1 illustrates the components of a typical large mainframe data base management system.

The *data definition language* is the vehicle for defining the content and form of the data base to the DBMS.

The *data directory* or *dictionary* is the repository of the *data base definition*.

The *data manipulation language* is used within programs to specify the update and retrieval operations to be

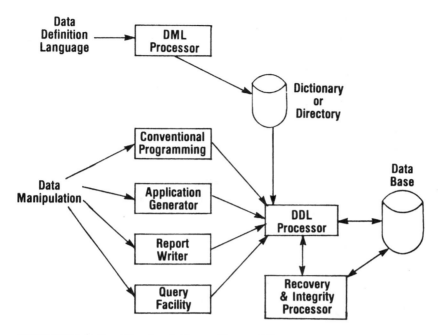

FIGURE 2.1 Typical Data Base Management System

performed by the DBMS. Usually it contains commands that allow one request to result in the retrieval or storage of many pieces of data.

Query and reporting facilities provide the means for accessing data without actual programming. These are becoming increasingly easy to use.

Application-generating tools permit construction of some programs without recourse to conventional programming techniques.

As a rule, the data manipulation language processors, query and reporting processors, and application-generating processors draw on the content of the directory or dictionary for definitions of the data and also for definitions of standard procedures for manipulating the data. As a result, repetitive redefinition of the data and procedures is minimized; sometimes it is eliminated.

Integrity routines protect the data base from the types of damage that might result when a number of different users or processes operate on it concurrently. They also provide for creation of back-up or safekeeping copies of the data, recording the effects of processing, and recreation of damaged data bases.[3]

Most data base management systems allow different users to be provided with different views of the data base. The definition of the overall data base is often referred to as a *schema*. The user views, which are usually a subset of the overall schema, are often referred to as *subschemas* or simply *views*. In another terminology, the schema is called the *internal model* and the subschema is called the *external model*.

Many data base management systems have evolved from relatively simple file-management routines. Today, a full-scale mainframe data base management system is a powerful tool for managing and manipulating data. Examples include Software AG's ADABASE, IBM's DB2, Burroughs's DMS, Univac's DMS, Cullinet's IDMS, Honeywell's IDS, IBM's IMS, SAS Institute's System 2000, and Cincom's Total. This is far from a complete list, and is not intended to be an endorsement or criticism of any product.

As a rule, the data base management systems available for microcomputers have fewer of these features and capabilities. They do, as a rule, provide more end user facilities, such as report writers, query languages, and graphics capabilities.

The typical data base management system is a powerful tool, but it is just that—a tool. Effective use of any tool requires knowledge and care. Many organizations have purchased data base management systems and undertaken large data base projects without proper training, analysis, planning, or user cooperation. The results have often been disastrous. Perhaps that is an overstatement, but a lot of time and money has been spent on projects that either were abandoned or did not produce the desired result. This comment is not a condemnation of data base management systems; it is an attempt to point out that large data base projects require considerable planning and care.

Other organizations have used a DBMS to implement separate systems that contain parochial views of the data and processing. The result has been to perpetuate the kind of systems architecture illustrated in Figure 1.2. There is nothing wrong with using the capabilities of a DBMS in the implementation of a limited system. In fact, just the facilities for error recovery, if used correctly, will surely enhance the quality of the system. *But, there must be problems if someone in the organization thinks that any systems which happen to access data via a DBMS are automatically components of an integrated data base system.* Nothing could be farther from the truth!

It would probably be foolish to attempt to construct any sort of integrated data base without a good DBMS, but that does not alleviate the need for analysis, planning, and design. In other words, while use of an adequate data base management system may be a necessary condition for the development of large, shared data bases, it is not a sufficient condition.

2.3 DATA DICTIONARIES

We have already defined a data dictionary or directory as the component of a DBMS which contains the description of the data base. It is possible to implement a data dictionary without using a DBMS to build data bases. It is also possible to place a lot more than just data base descriptions in a data dictionary. We will begin exploring these possibilities in detail in the next chapter. For now, let's just note that the data dictionary, like the DBMS, is a software tool. Effective use of this tool will help solve data-related problems, but the data dictionary is not a panacea.

2.4 FOURTH GENERATION TOOLS AND PROTOTYPING

The combination of DBMS, dictionary, and application or

program generator is often referred to as a *fourth generation tool*. Certain types of programs, particularly simple reports, inquiries, and updates can be developed very quickly *if the proper data base has been defined, created, and maintained, and if the dictionary has also been maintained correctly*. This has led to the practice of *prototyping*.

The idea of prototyping is that a programmer/analyst (or, as some would have it, an "applicationist") works with the end user to develop the reports and transactions more or less by trial and error. Results can be seen quickly. Desired changes can be made quickly. The goal is to shorten the lengthy process of analysis, program specification, and programming. This process encourages end user participation, so the final result is more likely to meet the end user's needs. Some make the assumption that once the desired result has been achieved, traditional programming techniques will be used to make the system more efficient. Others would argue that this should not be necessary. Employing these so-called fourth generation tools doesn't absolutely have to result in greater consumption of hardware resources, but it often does. You will have to decide for yourself if this will work in your shop.[4]

Prototyping has considerable promise, but it gives rise to problems. Programmers tend to consider a job done when the desired output is achieved. In data processing, we rarely go back and clean up something that works. We've looked at it enough to be tired of it. The users have other jobs they want done. Frequently the prototype becomes the production system. This can result in inefficient use of the hardware.

Another problem is that this development process may not provide for the same attention to all possibilities as conventional systems analysis techniques. The ease of change encourages a casual attitude. It is more likely that unanticipated problems will crop up after things have been running.

The prototyping process also encourages proliferation of unrelated, "single user" systems and data bases. This in turn may result in more redundancy, more synchronization problems, more undocumented data, and more problems for the organization.[5]

The biggest difficulties arise from the misapprehension that this type of software can eliminate the need for analysis and design. If the user and the "applicationist" do not understand the true nature of the data and processes, prototyping will merely provide a technique for creating the wrong report sooner. If the data base does not contain the needed data or allow access to the data, the report can never be produced. If the overall system design does not incorporate timely and accurate maintenance of the data, the reports will never be correct. If the data base is not efficiently designed, processing can never be efficient.[6]

This is not a condemnation of prototyping or the use of the fourth generation tools. It is a warning that this is a technical solution that can create as many problems as it solves if it is not applied with intelligence and care.

We might liken the use of fourth generation tools to alleviate programming drudgery to the use of robots to eliminate manual labor in a factory. In both cases, we facilitate the construction of something once we know what it is we want to construct and once we have assembled the necessary materials. In both cases we introduce efficiency and eliminate labor, but we accomplish this only if we conduct the requisite design and planning activities.

2.5 REUSABLE CODE

Reusable code is a special type of programmer productivity aid. To employ reusable code, the programmer constructs a library of standard routines that can be used in the development of many programs. The library is coupled with a system that allows a programmer to combine selected routines into the desired program.[7]

This technique formalizes a trick that programmers have used for years. It has considerable potential for increasing programmer output, but it is not a solution to our systems architecture problems. And, like prototyping, it isn't a substitute for analysis.

Reusable code can ensure consistency, reduce labor, and save time, but it is necessary to manage and maintain the library of reusable routines. Our comments regarding fourth generation tools also apply here.

2.6 INFORMATION CENTERS, PERSONAL COMPUTERS, AND DECISION SUPPORT SYSTEMS

The resources discussed in this section are all extensions of the fourth generation concept.

The information center is designed to make a computing facility directly available to the end user. The personal computer makes it possible for the end user to have the actual computer on his or her desk. Decision support systems are expected to fill the needs represented at the peak of the information triangle via the combination of readily accessible computing power and easy-to-use software tools.

Like the fourth generation concept, this constellation of resources has promise if used intelligently. However, it is frightening to think about what can happen if care is not taken. Many large corporations have purchased literally hundreds of personal computers. Talk about redundant data, duplication of effort, synchronization problems, and the like!

Beyond cost is the consideration, so easy to forget, that the beautiful report that has been prepared using some combination of spreadsheet and graph-drawing software is only as good as the analysis and data that went into producing it. How many end users really understand the inadequacies of the data extracted from mainframe systems? How many understand the implications of the statistical techniques buried in the software that draws those impressive graphs?

Large organizations can't control the data contained in a relatively small number of mainframe data bases. With the proliferation of personal computers, what is going to happen next?

2.7 DESIGN METHODOLOGIES

The converse of the preceding problem is the trend toward detailed design methodologies. Some of these are for sale. Some are available for the price of the books that contain them. Some have been developed internally by large corporations.

As a rule, these methodologies decompose the system development process into phases. Figure 2.2 illustrates a typical sequence of steps, including requirements definition, specification, technical definition, and programming. In effect, they document the techniques that successful analysts and systems designers have always used, provide a compendium of forms to use, and furnish a checklist that can be used to make sure nothing is overlooked.

FIGURE 2.2   Typical Design Cycle

Some methodologies consist mainly of a plan or sequence of steps. These might more properly be called life cycles. Others consist of specific analytic techniques, forms, and styles of documentation. Some are a combination of both.

Some of these methodologies may be too detailed to be workable. However, most provide for the selection of the subset of tasks appropriate to the job at hand.

Adherence to a sound design methodology can't help but improve the quality of the end product. Successful implementation of a computer system requires a precise definition of the functions to be performed and the data to be used. Any lack of understanding or ambiguity will be magnified by computerization. Careful planning has to produce a better end product than the haphazard approach. Most data processing development projects are undertaken to meet needs that are considered critical by the enterprise. There is almost always pressure from management to complete them in a hurry. In this situation, the natural human tendency is to start producing quickly. In the development of a complex system, this approach usually leads to overlooked details, the need to go back and do things over, missed schedules, and an inferior product. While the planning and analysis phases included in the typical methodology *seem* to take a lot of time at the beginning, the end result usually is a better product—and, that better product is, as a rule, produced sooner.

These assertions remain to be rigorously proven. To prove the efficacy of any given methodology, it would be necessary for the same project team to implement a given project in the same environment twice, with and without the methodology. However, it stands to reason that planning and an orderly approach will benefit any project. It is, of course, possible to pay lip service to a methodology, fill out all the right forms at the right times, but prevent it from serving its user effectively by gathering all the wrong information.

If a sound methodology is applied to the same limited views of business processes that resulted in the fragmented systems architecture we've been discussing, we will have improved the quality of the individual systems. But will we have eliminated redundant data, synchronization problems, inconsistent representations, and similar problems?

2.8 DATA MODELS, DATA BASE DESIGN METHODOLOGIES, AND DATA ARCHITECTURES

Data modelling is an important design technique. There are several different approaches. Each involves the substitution of formal analysis and documentation for the haphazard approach. Data modeling has the same relationship to data base design that a formal methodology has to system development.

The first thing we'd better do is think about the models in general. A model is "a representation, generally in miniature, to show the structure or serve as a copy of something."[8] In the data processing world, we frequently construct simulation models. These are special computer programs that contain a detailed description of the rules that govern some real-world system. We build these because it is very difficult to experiment with the real world. Designers of things like automobiles and airplanes use these models to try out possible design variations. The usual data model is different from a simulation model. *Data models are normally descriptive only.* We use them as tools to understand and describe things in the real world, but they are not suitable for simulation.

As is usually the case, there is a lot of terminology to learn in order to understand data modeling.

2.8.1 By the Way, What's an Architecture?

Lately, we've been hearing a lot about systems architectures and data architectures. What is the difference between a model and an architecture? We've already noted that a model is "a representation . . . to show the structure . . . of something." Well, architecture is "the design and structure of anything."[9]

Given this definition, the *data architecture* for a particular enterprise is the design and structure of that enterprise's data or data systems. Many organizations have considered it worthwhile to construct (or attempt to construct) a data model or a series of data models that illustrate or describe the data architecture.

Unfortunately, not everyone is careful about the use of these terms. Data models are sometimes called data architectures. All you can do about this is make sure you know what someone means when they use one of these words.

2.8.2 Types of Models

As Figure 2.3 indicates, there are several ways of classifying different types of data models.

	Hierarchical	Network	Relational
Physical			
Logical			
Conceptual			

FIGURE 2.3   Classifying Data Models

We can classify models according to *purpose*. The usual categories are physical, logical, and conceptual.

We can classify them according to *modelling technique or data structure* used. How does the model represent the data? The commonly encountered models are hierarchical, network, and relational.

There is also a special modelling technique referred to as entity-relationship modelling.

We'll briefly review each of these.[10]

Physical Model. The term *physical model* is used to describe the actual data representation used in the creation of a data base or file. The physical model describes the way the data is physically stored. The physical model for a complex data base will be very complex, because every detail must be included. It can be very difficult to see the relationship between the physical model and the data it contains.

A particular data base management system or file management technique will dictate the use of the particular modelling technique that forms the basis for that system. Thus, IBM's IMS system is based on the hierarchical model, while Cullinet's IDMS system is based on the network model.

The description of the whole data base, as we've already noted, is variously called the *schema* or the internal model. We've also noted that the description of the view or subset of the data base provided to a particular user or program is called a *subschema,* or an external model, or simply a view.[11]

Conceptual Model. Because the real content of a data base can be obscured by the elaborate detail of a physical model and because it is far from easy to select an appropriate physical model to suit a particular purpose, we often begin the data base design process by developing a *conceptual model.*

The conceptual model is a description of the actual data and the natural relationships found in that data. It is generally accepted that a good conceptual model should be meaningful to both the data base manager and the non-technical business person or end user. Therefore this type of model must be devoid of any reference to the technical details of a data base management system. It should, for example, show that an accounts payable system is concerned with vendors, invoices, checks, and the like. It should also show that vendors are described by such identifiers as names, addresses, and vendor numbers. A good conceptual model will provide a sound basis for subsequent physical data base design activities.[12]

As is the case with the physical model, any of the various modelling techniques may be used to construct the conceptual model. One significant difference is that the choice of conceptual model need not be determined by the choice of data base management system or file management technique. In fact, the data base management system to be used need not be known during the conceptual design phase. The conceptual model might well provide the basis for selecting the software.

The scope of the conceptual model is an important issue. It is reasonable to develop a conceptual model of the specific data to be processed by a distinct subsystem, such as accounts payable. This will surely improve the design of that system and provide a basis for understanding its data content and its relationship to other systems—but it will not solve our overall information architecture problems. Many have proposed the construction of a conceptual enterprise *schema* or data model showing all of an organization's data and all data relationships. This would certainly be useful, *but development of such a model is a major undertaking.* Many have started it; few, if any, have finished.

Logical Model. The logical model represents an intermediate step between the conceptual and the physical. Physical data base design activities involve detailed analysis of the data and its uses. The designer must know how many vendors, how many invoices, how many invoices per vendor, and so on. It is also necessary to analyze transactions, transaction volumes, and data requirements for each type of transaction. Many designers have found it useful to keep the conceptual model free of this sort of detail by developing a logical or intermediate model.

As is the case with the conceptual and physical models, any of the modelling techniques can be used in constructing a logical model. As is the case with the conceptual model, the modelling technique used need not match the structure of the data required by the data base management system.

The use of the logical model, the content of the logical model, and the relationship of the logical model to the physical model are still somewhat controversial. Most formal data base design methodologies employ some sort of logical model, but the style and content of this model varies greatly from method to method.[13]

Frequently, the logical model is *normalized*. This is a technical term for the result of a process that analyzes data elements and groups them together according to mathematical rules which ensure that each group of elements has an identifier that does uniquely identify that element grouping and no other. The formal theory of normalization is based on the formal mathematical theory of the *relational data model*. It is frequently couched in a mathematical terminology and notation which many people find forbidding. The basic concepts are not so difficult to understand once you get past the mathematics.[14]

Our observations regarding conceptual modelling are also true for logical modelling. Use of a logical model can significantly improve the system and data base design process. You may ask if this can be proven. Again, this assertion can't be formally proven like a mathematical theorem—but how would you hope to design a useful data base without an understanding of the data? *The logical model is merely documentation of the required understanding of the data, data identifiers, data relationships, volumes, uses, and so on.* Can recording this in a consistent, organized manner do anything but help? The logical model can also provide good documentation of the content of a data base. Of course, a logical modelling approach will not, by itself, solve all of our data problems.

Hierarchical Data Model. Figure 2.4 is an example of a hierarchical representation. This is easier to illustrate than to explain. The basic notion is that data groupings are arranged like an organization chart—a chart summarizing the accountability relationships within an organization such as the army, or the Roman Catholic Church. There is a so-called root grouping which is at the top of the structure and which forms the point of entry to the structure. Then there are one or more dependent groupings, each of which may have dependents.

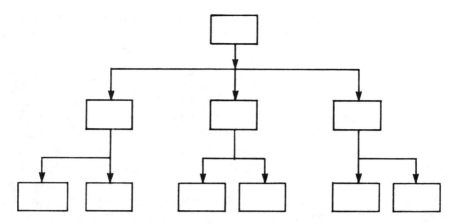

FIGURE 2.4   Hierarchical Structure

Data base management systems that make use of this structure frequently use a terminology that includes such words as *parent* data segments and *child* data segments. These words mean just what you think they should. Parents are closer to the top of the hierarchy. There are usually rigid rules stating that a particular type of group or segment can have but one parent segment type and a particular segment occurrence can have but one parent occurrence.[15]

The hierarchical model is useful because it is relatively easy to design a data base management system that makes use of it. It is particularly convenient if the data to be represented has a naturally hierarchical structure. If the data does not have such a structure, one must play some elaborate tricks in order to employ the hierarchical model. As an intellectual tool, this concept of data structure can be useful in the design of systems and data bases. By itself, it is not a solution to all of our data problems.

The Network Data Model. The network data model is another way of representing relationships among groupings of data. Once again, it is easier to illustrate than to explain. As Figure 2.5 shows, the main difference between the network and the hierarchical models is that there are fewer rules in the network model. A particular data grouping can have multiple owners. When this structure is represented by a diagram, the lines and arrows generally go in all possible directions. The conventional technique is to use an arrowhead to point from the owner or parent to the child or member.

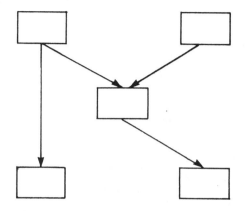

FIGURE 2.5   Network Structure

The network model, being more complex than the hierarchical model, is a little more difficult to build into a data base management system. However, it is sufficiently easy that it is used frequently. As a rule, a network model can be used to represent any structure that is naturally hierarchical and can also be used to represent more elaborate data interrelationships. As in the case of the hierarchical model, this concept of data structure can be a useful intellectual tool in the design of systems and data bases. By itself, it is not a solution to all of our data problems.

The CODASYL data model is a major subset of network data models.[16]

The Relational Data Model. The relational model is unique in that it has a firm theoretical foundation. There is a complete, and unfortunately imposing, mathematical theory of relations. In this context, the word *relation* has a special meaning. It refers to a particular grouping of data in a specific format. Once again, it is easier to illustrate than to explain. Data is viewed as organized into rows and columns as shown in Figure 2.6. Each row of a given relation consists of a similar group of data elements. These are commonly referred to as *tuples*. Each column is made up of elements of the same type. It is expected that all elements in a given column come from the same value set or *domain*. Several different columns may draw values from the same domain. (Think of a domain as the place where all the possible data values of a particular type live.)

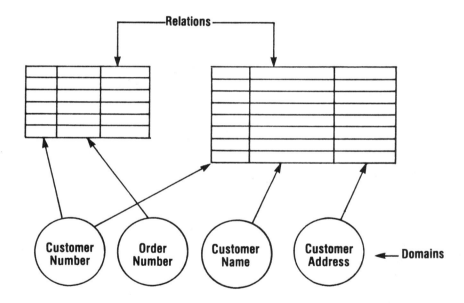

FIGURE 2.6   Relational Structure

There are well-defined operations that can be used to combine relations and select subsets of rows or columns from relations. The relational model and the families of operations called relational algebra and relational calculus have a property which mathematicians call *closure*. This means that given one or more correctly defined relations, application of the various relational operations will always result in correctly defined relations.

The relational model is more difficult to implement than the hierarchical or the network model. The emergence of workable data base management systems that make use of this model is a recent development. Most of these systems provide simpler data manipulation languages and query facilities than those incorporated in network or hierarchical systems. Many of these systems are based on the structured query language (SQL). This provides a degree of standardization that is surprising in the data processing industry.[17]

Current advertising for relational systems stresses ease of use. Most implementations of the relational model integrate the relational data base management system with other tools to form a fourth generation type of system. Many vendors of older data base management systems have developed interfaces that allow relational concepts and operations to be used against data structures that have been constructed using network or hierarchical data models.

Once again, as an intellectual tool, this concept of data structure can be extremely useful in the design of systems and data bases. By itself, it is not a solution to all of our data problems.

Entity Relationship Model. An entity relationship model is a representation of data in terms of entities, relationships, and attributes. Any object or concept of interest to the enterprise can be thought of as an *entity*. An entity is something that can be identified and defined, that is relevant to the project at hand, and about which data can be stored. It is a good idea to differentiate between specific *entity occurrences* and *entity sets*. The latter are types or categories. "Customer," in general, would be an entity set; "Customer 1234567" would be an entity occurrence within that set.

A *relationship* is a connection between two entities. Customers submit orders. Invoices are sent to customers. We might note that one customer can send many orders, that many invoices can be sent to one customer, that one invoice might relate to several orders. Again, it is worthwhile to distinguish between the set and a specific occurrence. Customer to order is a relationship set. Smith to order 2346 is an occurrence within that set. *Attributes* are those characteristics like name, date, and amount which describe entities or relationships. In the parlance of entity relationship modelling, an attribute is a field or data element that describes an entity or relationship.

An entity relationship model is usually represented by a network diagram such as Figure 2.7. There are a number of different styles of entity relationship modelling. Each has a specific terminology, set of rules, and collection of symbols. When someone shows you an entity relationship diagram, you need to take a few minutes to find out what the lines and arrows mean. An arrow might mean that one customer sends many orders. Or it might mean that an order cannot exist unless there is a customer who sent it. Entities or relationships might be represented by rectangles, diamonds, or circles, depending on the specifics of a particular technique.[18]

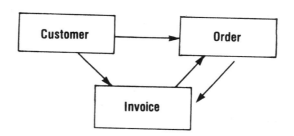

FIGURE 2.7   Entity Relationship Diagram

One of the biggest difficulties with entity relationship modelling arises from the fact that different people see the world differently. As a result, it frequently is not clear which should be entities, which should be relationships, and which should be attributes. An order might be thought of as an entity, or it might be thought of as a relationship between a customer and a product. One of these will seem more natural to you, but the other will seem more natural to someone else. If you insist that there can be but one perfect representation of the data, the arguments can be lengthy, acrimonious, and destructive. If your goal is to select from the possibilities a representation that will be useful to the enterprise and generally acceptable to all concerned, an entity relationship model can be an extremely useful tool.[19]

As you might expect, the entity relationship approach is primarily of use in the development of a conceptual data model. A given model might relate to a specific project, or it might relate to the entire enterprise. It's worth repeating that the development of an overall data model for a large enterprise is an extremely ambitious undertaking.

This is a tool that can help us understand the data well enough to resolve some of the organization's data problems, but it is not by itself a complete solution.

2.9 DATA BASE ADMINISTRATION AND DATA ADMINISTRATION

Most organizations have found the implementation of a large-scale data base management system in a mainframe environment to be a demanding and difficult task. The software generally provides numerous options that must be analyzed in relation to a particular environment. Control and maintenance of the software is complex and time-consuming. Design and tuning of large or complex data bases is demanding.

2.9.1 Data Base Administration

It is common practice to appoint a data base administrator to look after and coordinate these activities. Data base administration is frequently viewed as similar to systems programming, and staffed accordingly. Since many of the activities are highly technical, this is appropriate.

Typical data base administration activities include physical data base design, data base trouble shooting and error recovery, implementation of data security, and maintenance of DBMS software.[20]

2.9.2   Data Administration

More recently, there has been a growing recognition that effective use of data management software requires more than the solution of technical problems. Data base designs must be based on an understanding of the organization and its activities. Often the issues that must be resolved are more political than technical. Many organizations have recognized this and created a data base administration function charged with responsibility for the non-technical aspects of data management. Figure 2.8 is based on recommendations developed within the GUIDE organization.[21]

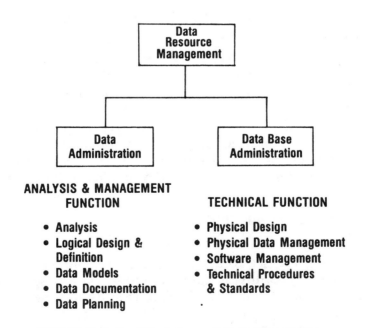

FIGURE 2.8   Division of Responsibility

Creation of a data administration function implies that an enterprise recognizes the existence of problems discussed in Chapter 1. It also implies that the enterprise recognizes that data is a valuable resource which needs to be administered and managed. This is a good start, but merely establishing the function on the organization chart does not guarantee solution of the problems. *Data administration is really a function of business management.* While it is closely related to data processing, it requires the participation and support of the user community.

A detailed discussion of the intricacies and requirements of data administration is beyond our scope here. We can note some typical goals, tools, and activities.

Typical Data Administration Goals. These are typical objectives for data administration:

Develop a unified, manageable, and readily usable data resource.

Catalogue and inventory the data resource. Document its uses.

Eliminate unnecessary and unplanned redundancy.

Eliminate unnecessary data transfers.

Provide for timeliness and availability of data.

Improve the maintainability of data bases and systems.

Improve the system development process.

Typical Data Administration Tools. These are the tools that the data administrator typically employs:

Data and business models

Data dictionary

Data base management system

Standards and procedures

Naming conventions

Typical Data Administration Activities. These are typical data administration activities:

Development of data models that document types of data, sources and uses of data, and the relationship between data and business processes.

Development of a data dictionary that documents specific formats, usages, and locations of data.

Standardization of data naming, formats, definitions, and coding structures.

Documentation of data security requirements. Development and enforcement of data security procedures.

Control of versions of systems and data bases.

Unfortunately, the data administrator often gets bogged down in day-to-day technical details and is unable to deal adequately with the bigger and longer range issues.[22]

Many of these topics are discussed again in Chapters 7 through 11.

2.10 PURCHASED PACKAGES

Many organizations have attempted to solve their software development problems by purchasing software. This approach is usually expected to eliminate development costs and speed implementation. Some benefit can be gained by purchasing software, but several caveats are in order. First, while programming may be eliminated, planning and analysis will not be. Extensive analysis is required to identify the organization's needs and decide whether the proposed purchase will meet the requirements.

Many contemporary software systems provide numerous options so that they can be used by a variety of organizations. In some cases, there are so many options that the software package resembles a very high level language. Implementation of this type of purchase clearly requires analysis to determine which options should be selected. Specifying the options can be a major effort. It is essential both to document the options selected and to control the choice and modification of selections.

Many organizations have fallen into the trap of making extensive modifications to purchased software. Frequently this not only invalidates any warranty but also complicates or even precludes migration to improved versions of the software.

Finally, purchasing software may do nothing to solve the inconsistencies, redundancies and other problems we've been discussing. It is likely to be helpful only if several packages are purchased from a single vendor and that vendor has taken care to truly integrate the various components.

None of these observations is intended as an out-and-out condemnation of purchased packages. They are merely a warning. Excellent results can be achieved if software is purchased and installed carefully.

2.11 SUMMARY

The various tools and techniques discussed in this chapter constitute the data administrator's bag of tricks. Taken together with an organization's willingness to invest in long-term solutions to data problems, they offer the possibility of greatly improving the quality of data available for managing and operating any enterprise.

It is very important to realize that many data problems are organizational or political. *A web of separate systems, with all its redundancies and inconsistencies, comes into being because of the distinct and inconsistent views of the enterprise and its data held by various people.* Usually the complex of inconsistent systems represents an organization's inconsistent view of itself. Separate copies of the same data are created because people want to control their own copies of things. Changing the systems architecture may necessitate changing the organization. If a proposed solution does not take this into consideration, it is not a solution and cannot succeed.

The available technology can really help in solving the problems that we've been discussing. However, technical solutions that do not recognize practical political realities are doomed to failure.[23]

Now that the stage has been set, the remainder of this book will discuss data dictionaries and their uses.

NOTES

1. GUIDE is an independent organization of users of IBM mainframe computers. Meetings are normally attended by several thousand representatives of various IBM customers. Committees work on selected problems and present the results of their work at general sessions. GUIDE and the companion organization, SHARE, provide excellent forums on current issues in information processing.

2. Here are three references that discuss the possibilities and problems of data bases in large organizations: James Martin, *Managing the Data Base Environment* (Englewood Cliffs, N.J.: Prentice-Hall, 1983) and *Strategic Data-Planning Methodologies* (Englewood Cliffs, N.J.: Prentice-Hall, 1982); and Mark L. Gillenson and Robert Goldberg, *Strategic Planning, Systems Analysis, and Database Design: The Continuous Flow Approach* (New York: John Wiley & Sons, 1984).

3. For a detailed discussion of these technical issues, see C. J. Date, *An Introduction to Database Systems,* Vol. 2 (Reading, Mass: Addison-Wesley, 1983).

4. For a comprehensive discussion of prototyping, see Bernard H. Boar, *Application Prototyping* (New York: John Wiley & Sons, 1984).

5. From James Martin, *System Design from Provably Correct Constructs* (Englewood Cliffs, N.J.: Prentice-Hall, 1985): "The evidence with the use of nonprocedural languages in commercial DP indicates that thorough data-base administration is a vital key to their success. They make systems development easier than with traditional programming and it is only too easy for developers serving a particular user group to develop their own data, ignoring the needs of other users. A Tower of Babel grows up in the data if a data administration [sic] does not have firm control."

6. Ibid. "Ill-conceived requirements or misstated requirements [can] lead to correctly-meshing mechanisms for executing those wrong requirements."

7. For the original definition of reusable code, see Robert G. Lanergan and Bryan A. Poynton, *Reusable Code: The Application Development of the Future* (Burlington, Mass: Raytheon Company, 1979).

8. It's often a good idea to look in a dictionary and find out what other people might mean by a particular term. In this case, the reference is *The Random House Dictionary* (New York: Ballantine Books, 1978).

9. Ibid.

10. You will find more details about all of this in any good text on data base. Particularly recommended are I. T. Hawryszkiewicz, *Database Analysis and Design* (Chicago: Science Research Associates, 1984) and S. Atre, *Data Base: Structured Techniques for Design, Performance, and Management* (New York: John Wiley & Sons, 1980). Hawryszkiewicz provides a very complete survey of conceptual modelling techniques. Atre provides several complete examples which proceed from conceptual modelling through physical design.

11. Sometimes a data base management system will use one model for the physical or internal view and another for the external or user view. Several systems now provide relational views that are derived from hierarchical or network storage techniques.

12.   For a comprehensive discussion of conceptual modelling, see Hawryszkiewicz, op cit.

13.   For a comprehensive discussion of logical modelling, see Hawryszkiewicz, op cit.

14.   For a good (and not too difficult) explanation of the basics of normalization, see William Kent, "A Simple Guide to Five Normal Forms in Relational Database Theory," *Communications of the ACM,* February 1983.

15.   Here's a concept that will come up again later on. We need to differentiate types or classifications that are generalizations from specific occurrences. For example, customer is a generalization. XYZ Company is a specific occurrence. Customer address is a generalization. 123 Main Street is a specific occurrence. A lot of data base design issues can be very confusing if you don't keep this clearly in mind.

16.   See the *CODASYL Data Base Task Group 1971 Report* (New York: Association for Computing Machinery, 1971).

17.   See, for example, C. J. Date, *An Introduction to DB2* (Reading, Mass.: Addison-Wesley, 1984).

18.   See Peter Chen, *The Entity-Relationship Approach to Logical Data Base Design* (Wellesley, Mass.: QED Information Sciences, Inc., 1977).

19.   It really isn't possible to design an adequate system or data base unless there is thorough understanding of the business data involved. It is possible for a really good analyst to keep the details of a relatively small system in his or her head and develop a decent design. As the problem and the project team increase in size, this becomes harder and harder to do. Conceptual modelling is a tool for formalizing the understanding of the business data and documenting it so that everyone involved can understand it.

Some of the modelling techniques are much more elaborate and sophisticated than others. The more elaborate techniques really can lead to better designs because they provide richer, more complete ways of describing things. *Unfortunately, too much emphasis on technique can result in too little emphasis on the business understanding. It is probably more important to adopt a modelling technique that everyone involved can understand than to try to chose one that provides perfection.* It seems important, in any large project, to have a relatively simple conceptual description of the data objects involved. You would be wise to save the more sophisticated and complex techniques for the logical or intermediate model and keep the conceptual model simple.

20. For a discussion of current practices in data base administration, see B. Kahn and L. Garceau, "A Developmental Model of the Database Administration Function," *Journal of Management Information Systems* 1 (Spring 1985), pp. 87-101.

21. See the GUIDE paper, *Data Administration Methodology* (Chicago, Ill.: GUIDE International Corporation, 1978).

22. See Mark L. Gillenson, "The State and Practice of Data Administration—1981," *Communications of the ACM,* , Vol. 25, No. 10, October 1982; and Beverly K. Kahn, "Some Realities of Data Administration," in *Communications of the ACM,* October 1983.

23. The author's initial formal introduction to data concepts was a class conducted by Leo Cohen, founder of Performance Development Corporation and author of several books on data base. He made the very appropriate comment that the would-be data (base) administrator might best begin by studying Machiavelli.

3 Basic Dictionary Concepts

This chapter discusses basic dictionary concepts, provides some definitions, and serves as an introduction to the remainder of the book.

3.1 WHAT IS A DATA DICTIONARY?

Data dictionary has become another one of those terms that must be used with care because it is used to mean so many different things. The basic idea is simple enough: a *data dictionary* is an organized reference to the data content of something. That something could be a program, a system, a data base, or a collection of all the files, programs, systems, data bases, and manual records maintained by a large corporation.

A data dictionary may be maintained manually or it may be a computerized data base. Sometimes the term is used to refer to a software product that is utilized to maintain a dictionary data base. We'll clarify this in the remainder of the chapter.

3.2   WHY HAVE A DATA DICTIONARY?

People who are learning to write computer programs often get into trouble by forgetting which name has been assigned to which piece of data. (If you haven't learned programming and this statement doesn't mean much to you, read note 1.) In this case, the solution is simple: a programmer should make a list of names and what they will stand for before writing any program code. Ideally, this list should be included as comments in the data definition portion of the program. Programming languages that require a formal set of data declarations remind the programmer of this necessity. Most people who still write any programs or who are closely associated with people who write them also know that there is a great temptation to ignore this simple step. "After all, there will only be ten or twenty data names in this program. I'm certainly intelligent enough to make the names up as I go along and remember which is which."

Some language processing systems provide a cross-reference listing which shows all uses within a given program of each name. This can be a big help to a programmer. Such a listing does not, however, show definitions.

Similarly, anyone who has been involved in the design and implementation of a large system has had the opportunity to encounter all sorts of data-related problems. *If the people who will be using the system and the analysts and the programmers don't all share a common understanding of the data, the system may never work correctly.*

The human mind is very flexible. We make interpretations and adjustments without thinking about it. You know that postal code, zip, and zip code all mean pretty much the same thing. If you generally use one term and I use another, you will probably be able to interpret what I'm trying to tell you. The computer is not gifted with this ability to interpret. A particular computer program will embody a very specific set of assumptions about a piece of data and that's it. A zip code is a five-digit numeric data item. It will appear in packed decimal format in the twenty-seventh through twenty-ninth positions of the input record.

Now for some of the problems. What if you want to record an address in Canada and include the Canadian postal code? It has six characters and can consist of numerals and letters. What happens when zip codes become nine digits? Suppose you want to move the zip code over five places to make room for an extra-long city name like Truth or Consequences, New Mexico? Too bad. You've got to change the programs or it just can't be done. If several different programs process the same file of data records, each program must be written with precisely the same understanding of the size, location, format, and content of every piece of data. It is a common practice to create a single library of data file definitions, which are then copied into all programs in a system to alleviate this problem. The usual term for this is *copy library*. This bit of technology does not completely solve the problem. If there are many different copy libraries, or if there are no procedures to ensure that the proper copy libraries are used and kept up to date, there will still be problems.

At any rate, because of these and other similar pitfalls, more and more people accept the need for an organized approach to system design and development. Notice that this is not restricted to wholly computerized systems. Most system development methodologies that have been proposed recommend formal specifications of data items, data files, and reports. These specifications include names, descriptions, definitions, and so on. This might cover all data processed by a single program, all data processed by a system or collection of programs, or all data used in conducting the business of a large corporation. It has become common practice to call the reference that is developed a *data dictionary*.[2]

3.3   THE CONCEPT OF METADATA

In the broadest sense, a data dictionary is any organized

collection of information about data. It is currently fashionable to use the word *metadata* to indicate that a higher-than-usual level of abstraction is involved, that the reference is not to plain ordinary data: Metadata is data about data.

Take a look at Figure 3.1. Any information system, whether or not it is computerized, exists to store and process data about real-world objects—customers and invoices, for example. The illustration indicates specific customers, identified by names like John J. Johnson and Melvin M. Melvin. There are also specific invoices, identified by numbers like 123456 and 654321. As an analytic device, we differentiate the specific entity occurrences *Johnson* and *123456* from the entity types or entity sets *customer* and *invoice*. (Entity and relationship sets are discussed in Chapter 2.) Then we create data records that will represent the entity occurrences. We define specific record types to represent specific entity types. We will probably call them customer records and invoice records. Frequently, we also assign keys or identifiers such as customer name and invoice number to differentiate one record occurrence from another.

A data dictionary can be designed to contain data about those customer and invoice record types. We identify an entity type called *record* and populate our dictionary with record occurrences that represent the customer record, the invoice record, and any others we might have. Notice that the record name would make a good key or identifier in this case.

The customer and invoice records in the data base contain ordinary data. The "record" records in the dictionary contain metadata, data about data. Some people have even started to talk about *metametadata*. Let's leave that idea alone.

3.4   THE NEED FOR AN AUTOMATED DICTIONARY

If you should set out to document and index all the data processed by a complex system, or all the data referenced in the day-to-day operation of a large organization, you would very quickly discover that populating a dictionary involves a

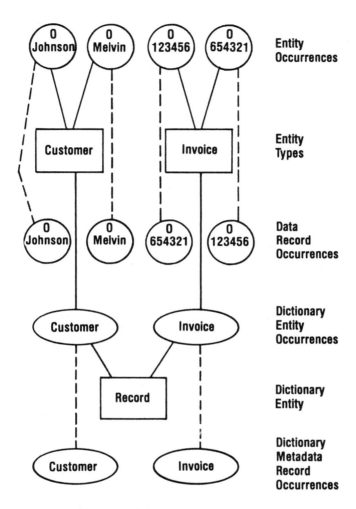

FIGURE 3.1   Metadata

lot of clerical effort. This is the type of activity that can be facilitated by the introduction of a well-designed computer system. It is not surprising that a number of software products have been developed for the purpose of creating and maintaining a data dictionary. What is such a software product usually called? You guessed it: *a data dictionary is also a software product that has been developed for the purpose of creating and maintaining metadata or data about data. It might be thought of as a DBMS designed for metadata.*

It is also pretty common to use the term data dictionary to refer to the computer data base containing the metadata, or to the combination of the dictionary software and the data.

Thus, a data dictionary is also a computerized data base of metadata, or data about data, together with the software and procedures used to create and maintain the dictionary data base.

3.5   DICTIONARY AND DBMS INTERRELATIONSHIPS

3.5.1   Dictionary Dependence on a DBMS

Today, most vendors of data base management systems also provide data dictionary products. Not surprisingly, the data dictionary furnished by a particular vendor almost always makes use of the vendor's data base management system for management of the dictionary data base. A data dictionary tends to require a complex data structure that can be more easily manipulated via a data base management system. In addition, the facilities for journalling, error recovery, and auditing provided by the typical DBMS are very important to the designer of a data dictionary. This means that you may have to install a DBMS in order to install a dictionary. It also means that if you already have a DBMS, your choice of dictionary may be very restricted. Each selection is related to the other.

3.5.2   DBMS Dependence on a Dictionary

In some cases, the data base management system also makes use of some of the data in the dictionary, and neither can function without the other. The reasoning is that since the DBMS must have access to a description of the data base, there might as well be one shared copy. The elimination of redundancy is advantageous, but the dependency of the DBMS on the data dictionary can cause operational problems. (These are discussed in greater detail in Section 3.8 and also in Chapter 8.)

Thus, a data dictionary is also that component of an integrated data base management system which contains and maintains the definition and description of the data and the data base.

3.6   DICTIONARY OR DIRECTORY?

Data directory is another term that is frequently used. As a rule, a dictionary is a book of words, arranged alphabetically with meanings, while a directory is an alphabetical list of names and addresses. Some software vendors use the terms interchangeably; some consistently use one or the other. When there is a distinction, directory usually refers to a definition or map of data stored on the computer. This includes actual record and file definitions. A dictionary can contain a lot more.

In other words, *a data directory is a machine-readable definition of a computerized data base.* It is often used by a data base management system to obtain the sizes, formats, and locations of data records and fields. *A data dictionary is a superset that can contain additional data and definitions.*

Some vendors of data base management systems now use the term *catalog* instead of directory or dictionary. This usually means that there is a repository of metadata which is more extensive than the usual directory but not as elaborate as a dictionary.

3.7   AGAIN, WHAT IS A DATA DICTIONARY?

At about this point, you'd be justified in saying, "Please, cut out the fooling around and give me one good definition of data dictionary!" Unfortunately, each of the above is a valid definition based on current usage. You need to keep them all in mind and determine from the context what is meant in a particular instance. *In this book, the term data dictionary means the computerized dictionary data base plus the software and procedures.*

3.8 ACTIVE VERSUS PASSIVE DICTIONARIES

Dictionaries are often categorized as active or passive. This refers to the extent of integration with the data base management system. If the dictionary and the DBMS are integrated to the extent that the DBMS uses the definitions in the dictionary at run time, the dictionary can be said to be very *active*. (If you aren't sure of the difference between compile time and run time, see note 3.) If the dictionary is free-standing or independent of the DBMS, it can be said to be *passive*.

An active dictionary must contain an accurate, up-to-date description of the physical data base in order for the data base management system to access the data. There is but one machine-readable definition that is shared by all software components. The Cullinet Integrated Data Dictionary, described in Chapter 4, is a good contemporary example of this.

Given a passive dictionary, there are multiple definitions. The definition used by the DBMS is separate and distinct from that contained in the dictionary and possibly from those used by various programs. The IBM DB/DC Data Dictionary, described in Chapter 5, is a good example of this. As usual, there can be a difference of opinion about this. The IBM dictionary will generate the definitions and control blocks that are used by the DBMS. It can also be used as a programmer's copy library for standard data definitions. For these reasons, promotional literature states that the IBM dictionary is active. Since there is no direct link and there are usually two copies of the data base description, let's call this a relatively passive system or perhaps a hybrid active/passive dictionary. Obviously, it is more active than some and less passive than others. MSP's DATAMANAGER, which is discussed in Chapter 6, is an example of a passive system. Figures 3.2, 3.3, and 3.4 illustrate the three possibilities.

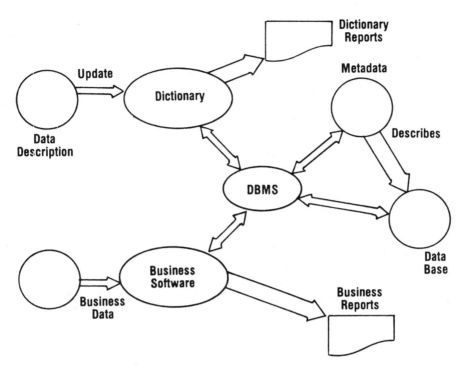

FIGURE 3.2   Active Dictionary

A more active dictionary is desirable for a number of reasons. There is only one definition of a data base to store; there is only one definition to maintain. It is not possible, therefore, to have one definition in one place and another definition in the other place. If, on the other hand, the dictionary is passive or relatively passive, more storage space is required, there is some duplication of effort in maintaining the two copies of the same data, and great care must be taken to ensure that the two definitions are actually identical. This is always a problem when redundancy exists. Be sure to note, by the way, that the existence of a single dictionary description of the physical data base does not guarantee that the description and the actual data base match.

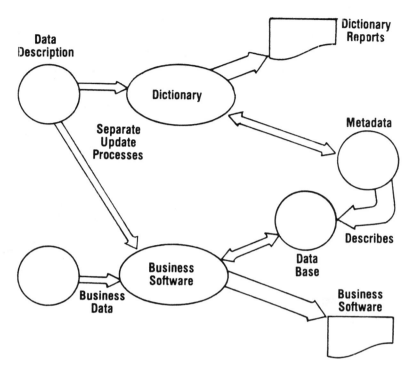

FIGURE 3.3 Passive Dictionary

Elimination of redundancy can be a mixed blessing, however. When the operation of production systems is completely
dependent on the dictionary, the dictionary must be maintained and protected with great care. If many programs need
concurrent access to a single dictionary, interesting performance problems can arise. If programmers doing program
development work must also access that same dictionary, this
problem will be compounded.

Both the tightly coupled approach exemplified by Cullinet
and the loosely coupled approach exemplified by IBM have
their benefits and drawbacks. Figure 3.5 is a table of advantages and disadvantages. Chapters 4, 5, and 6 clarify this by
discussing specific dictionary products.

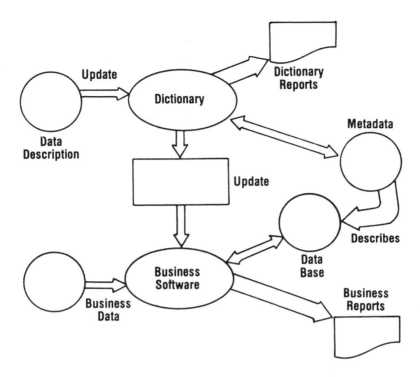

FIGURE 3.4   Hybrid or Active/Passive Dictionary

ACTIVE	**PASSIVE**
One Copy of Definition	Redundant Definitions
	– Inconsistency possible
	– Multiple maintenance required
	– Additional storage required
Production Systems Depend on Dictionary Availability	Production Systems Unaffected by Dictionary Failures
Dictionary Can Become a Bottleneck	One System Does Not Affect Another

FIGURE 3.5   Active Versus Passive Dictionaries

One argument in favor of a completely passive dictionary is that many installations utilize a data base management system for some processing and conventional access methods for others. Some installations even make use of more than one DBMS. Also, many installations fulfill some of their data processing needs by purchasing software packages. These frequently use unique data definition and management techniques. In this situation, effective data resource management requires careful planning and good procedures. Chapters 7, 8, and 10 show you how to develop appropriate procedures for your shop.

3.9 DICTIONARY CONTENT

If you wanted to design a data dictionary system and the associated dictionary data base, how would you go about it? You might begin by identifying 'he entities or objects of interest, the relationships between various entities, the attributes or descriptors of the entities and relationships, and the processing and reporting to be accomplished. The data content of a dictionary data base is discussed in detail in Chapters 4, 5, 6, 7, 8, and 10. For now, just assume that you would probably want to include individual data elements (fields), collections of data elements (records), and collections of records (files). You might also decide to include programs and collections of programs (systems). For a typical example of this, see Figure 3.6. This is a very simple form of entity relationship diagram. Entities are shown as rectangles. Relationships are shown as lines connecting the rectangles. An arrowhead designates the "many" side of a one-to-many or many-to-many relationship. We will use this type of model frequently in this book. If you were designing a dictionary data base to be used with a specific data base management system, you would want to be sure that your basic definitions were compatible with that DBMS. *The designers of most existing data dictionary systems seem to have done something like this.*

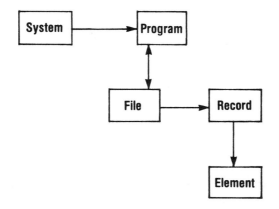

FIGURE 3.6   Typical Dictionary Entities

3.10 EXTENSIBILITY

A detailed review of available data dictionary packages also reveals that each designer or design team had some unique ideas about what should or should not be included. Chapters 4, 5, 6, 7, and 8 give you an indication of this. The reason is that data processing and systems design are evolving disciplines, and there are a lot of different ideas about how things should be done. In fact, if you review any dictionary system and start to think about how you would use it, you will find yourself saying, ''I'd sure like to add and modify some things here.'' Recognizing this, the designers of many of the dictionary packages have provided *extensibility*. This means that the software can more or less change itself. You are given the ability to add entity types, descriptions, and relationships. This is a very important feature. You will see that in Chapters 7 and 10.

3.11   UPDATE AND REPORTING

Obviously, a collection of metadata is useful only if you can get at it and use it. This is true of any collection of any kind of data. So, all dictionary systems incorporate some means for update and some kind of reporting. There are two problems with the reporting subsystems included in most packages. First, the reports are designed by technicians for technicians. As a result, they aren't always easy to read and some of the things on them only mean something to a person who really understands the inner workings of the dictionary software. Second, the standard reports don't provide well for anything added by means of extensibility features. So, many users design and create their own custom reports. Most packages provide some vehicle for accomplishing this. Most of the up-to-date packages also provide for on-line inquiry and updating. This is a very important feature. Many batch-oriented dictionary implementations have failed because the update process was just too tedious. A data dictionary, like any other data base, must be maintained to be useful.

3.12   ONE LAST TIME: WHAT IS A DATA DICTIONARY?

With the advent of extensibility and customized reporting, the typical data dictionary has become a generalized data base system that can be used for a lot more than the original designers ever anticipated. Thus, a data dictionary is a system for maintaining data about data (metadata). Vendor-supplied packages provide for a variety of basic data-oriented objects such as field, record, and program. Provision is made for entry and reporting of this metadata. The user can customize most of these systems via extensibility and user-written reports. Dictionaries are classified as active or passive according to the degree of integration with an associated data base management system.

3.13 ONE MORE COMPLICATION: PACKAGES AND TOOLS HAVE DICTIONARIES

Many of the complex software packages, such as those discussed in Section 2.10, come with built-in data dictionaries. Most of the fourth generation tools alluded to in Section 2.4 also have built-in dictionaries. Sometimes the vendors call these directories or catalogs.

Some of these are very simple and might properly be classified as directories. Some are quite extensive. Most concentrate on data-related entities, such as elements and records. Few provide extensibility. As a general rule, these are not comprehensive enough for use as an organization's primary or master data dictionary. However, it is important to be aware of the existence of each of these repositories of metadata. They cannot be eliminated because the associated software products will not operate without them. Care must be exercised to ensure that all dictionaries, directories and catalogs are maintained in a consistent manner.

3.14 LOOKING AHEAD

The next three chapters discuss representative data dictionary systems—the Integrated Data Dictionary marketed by Cullinet Database Systems, the DB/DC Dictionary marketed by the IBM Corporation, and DATAMANAGER, marketed by MANAGER Software Products. These are discussed because they illustrate typical data dictionary systems, they illustrate different implementation concepts, they are widely marketed, and they happen to be the those with which the author is most familiar. Do not take this as an endorsement of these products or a criticism of others.[4]

NOTES

1. All data processed by a computer has to be stored inside the computer. Each memory location has a unique address. These addresses are analogous to the numbers on post office boxes. The numbering scheme varies from computer to computer because it is highly dependent on the unique hardware architecture. Just about all modern programming systems provide for reference to data via symbolic names. This means that instead of remembering that the customer name is 35 characters of information stored at location 2,306,170 a programmer can assign a name like CUST–NAME or ITEM27 and allow the system to do the actual address arithmetic. This is a great labor-saving device.

2. For example, see Chris Gane and Trish Sarson, *Structured Systems Analysis: Tools and Techniques* (Englewood Cliffs, N.J.: Prentice-Hall, 1979).

3. Many system design and programming problems revolve around the concepts of time and binding. At one point in time, a designer or programmer develops concepts and procedures for a program or data file. At a later time, this definition is entered into a computer in some well-defined format. Finally, some sort of compiler intercepts the definition and produces machine instructions that the computer hardware will follow. This is often referred to as *compile time*. Finally, there is a time at which the actual data processing occurs. This is often referred to as *run time*. In a complex system there must be a time at which a number of separately created definitions are bound together. A highly active dictionary will provide the potential for deferring the program to data base binding until the last possible minute. A late binding time is generally considered desirable because it provides flexibility. Late binding usually requires the use of more system resources. It also makes careful housekeeping a necessity.

4. The following sources describe the features of products that are currently available: H. Lefkovits, E. Sibley, and S. Lefkovits, *Information Resource/Data Dictionary Systems* (Wellesley, Mass.: QED Information Sciences, Inc., 1983), Chs. 1,2; F. Allen, M. Loomis, and M. Mannino, ''The Integrated Dictionary/Directory System,'' *ACM Computing Surveys* 14 (June 1982); Belkis W. Leong-Hong and Bernard K. Plagman, *Data Dictionary/Directory Systems: Administration, Implementation, and Usage* (New York: John Wiley & Sons, 1982); J. Van Duyn, *Developing a Data Dictionary System* (Englewood Cliffs, N.J.: Prentice-Hall, 1982); and Ronald G. Ross, *Data Dictionaries and Data Administration* (New York: AMACOM, 1978).

4 The Cullinet Integrated Data Dictionary

This chapter discusses Cullinet's Integrated Data Dictionary in order to illustrate some things about data dictionaries in general. Words such as PROGRAM are capitalized when they are used in the context of IDMS or Integrated Data Dictionary keywords. They are not capitalized when they are used in a more ordinary sense.

4.1 AN IMPORTANT WARNING

Although this chapter contains material on the philosophy, features, and use of the Cullinet Integrated Data Dictionary, it is not a substitute for careful reading of the technical manuals provided by the vendor. New versions of this software are always being developed. There is no way to guarantee that the version that will be current when you read this book will not be significantly different from the version that was current when the book was written. This is particularly true of the Cullinet product line; Cullinet has announced a number of significant enhancements and additions in recent years.

Also, since our purpose is to illustrate dictionary features and their use rather than to provide a definitive reference for a particular product, details are sometimes omitted. Emphasis is placed on the logic of the system, not on technical implementation details. A data dictionary is a complex system, and technical system details are important, but it is very easy to get lost in technical details and forget what the system and processing are really about. For all of these reasons, be sure to read the vendor's technical manuals thoroughly and attend appropriate training classes before attempting to use the Cullinet dictionary.

4.2   THE INTEGRATED DATA DICTIONARY

The Cullinet Integrated Data Dictionary is an example of a highly *active* dictionary. It is designed as the central component of an integrated family of products which includes the dictionary itself, IDMS/R, IDMS–DB, IDMS–DC, Culprit, On-Line Query, Application Development System On-Line, Application Development System Batch, Information Data Base, GOLDENGATE, and Automatic System Facility. Figure 4.1 illustrates this integrated architecture.

4.3   The IDMS FAMILY

The dictionary will be easier to understand after a brief discussion of each of the other members of the family.

IDMS and IDMS/R. The original IDMS, the Integrated Database Management System marketed by Cullinet Database Systems, is an implementation of the CODASYL (Conference on Data Systems Languages) model for data base management

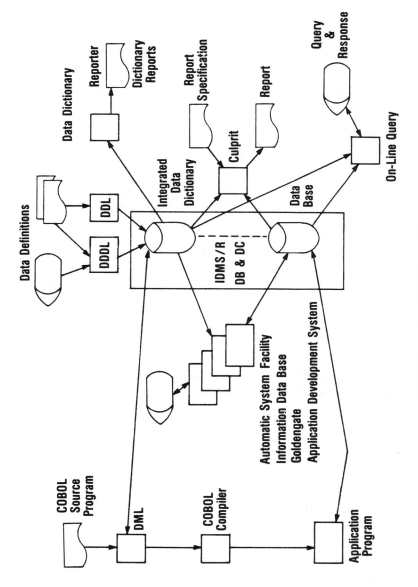

FIGURE 4.1 IDMS Architecture

systems.[1] As such, the system provides a COBOL-like Data Manipulation Language and a network Data Model. The newer release, IDMS/R, or IDMS relational, incorporates features of the *relational model*. Thus, a contemporary IDMS implementation is a combination of the network data model with relational concepts. The underlying physical data base is usually implemented via the network model. Programs and users are provided with views based on both the relational model and the network model.

The basic CODASYL IDMS system is a designer-oriented data base management system. That is, it is intended for use by systems development professionals who are prepared to spend significant amounts of time in highly structured design and implementation activities. IDMS/R, on the other hand provides features of end-user-oriented data base management systems. In other words, simple systems that do not have high performance requirements can be developed on a trial and error basis. However, it might be necessary to redesign, redefine, and reimplement the physical data base to achieve desirable performance. This can sometimes be done without any impact on the programs and users.

As Figure 4.2 illustrates, an IDMS network data base is defined in terms of Records and Sets. It is important to understand a little about this, because the Cullinet Dictionary is actually an IDMS data base. A Record is a collection of Fields or Data Elements that can be stored or retrieved as a unit. A Set is a relationship between Record types. A Set type consists of a single Owner Record type and one or more Member Record types. It is necessary to differentiate between a Record type and specific Record occurrences and between a Set type and specific Set occurrences.

Most IDMS documentation uses a combination of Bachman diagrams and occurrence diagrams to clarify these distinctions. The Bachman diagram is a sort of entity relationship diagram, named after Charles Bachman, one of the pioneers of the CODASYL concept. Such documentation is common for CODASYL systems. The Bachman diagram illustrates the record and relationship types defined for the data base. The occurrence diagram illustrates representative record and relationship

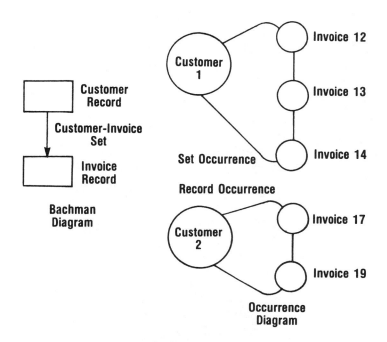

FIGURE 4.2   IDMS Set Relationship

occurrences. The data manipulation language provides commands for storing or retrieving a Record occurrence based on its own identity or on its role as either the Owner or a Member of a particular Set occurrence.

The definition of an entire CODASYL Data Base is usually referred to as a SCHEMA or a SCHEMA definition. This consists of the appropriate Record and Set descriptions. IDMS, along with most CODASYL data base management systems, provides a COBOL-like Data Definition Language (DDL) that is used to describe the SCHEMA.

As illustrated in Figure 4.3, the CODASYL framework allows an individual Program or User to be given a unique view of the data base. This is referred to as a SUBSCHEMA. A Record type defined in a SUBSCHEMA may consist of all the fields or elements defined for the corresponding SCHEMA

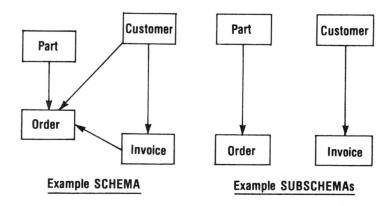

FIGURE 4.3   SCHEMA and SUBSCHEMA

Record type, or it may consist of some subset of these fields. The SUBSCHEMA version cannot contain data that is not in the SCHEMA. The SUBSCHEMA may contain all of the Record and Set types defined for the SCHEMA or some subset of them.

The SCHEMA/SUBSCHEMA concept allows a measure of program/data independence. The so-called Logical Record Facility allows a SUBSCHEMA Record type to consist of one or more SCHEMA Record types, provided that a path of Set relationships can be defined from Record to Record in the SCHEMA (see Figure 4.4). This is a powerful extension to the CODASYL model. IDMS/R extends this concept to provide a relational data base view.

A CODASYL data base is subdivided into Areas. These are similar to the Files in a conventional file-oriented environment. Cullinet has added a Device Media Control Language (DMCL) that provides flexible mapping from Areas to operating system Files (or data sets).

IDMS–DB is the system component that manages such functions as data base access, record protection, error recovery, journalling, and other housekeeping functions. IDMS–DC is the system component that manages communications. IDMS–DB and IDMS–DC are integrated into a single component that is referred to as the Central Version.

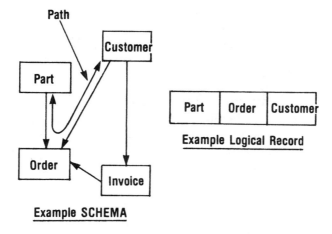

FIGURE 4.4 Logical Record Facility

Culprit. Culprit is the report writer associated with IDMS. It is able to make use of the data definitions contained in the dictionary. Relatively simple descriptions of the desired output will result in the production of a printed report. Little programming, as such, is required.

OLQ. On-Line Query allows direct access to the IDMS Data Manipulation Language from a terminal. This provides the sophisticated user with a vehicle for ad hoc or extemporaneous queries. Programmers and data base administrators will find many uses for OLQ. Recent releases incorporate a simplified query language that can be used by sophisticated end users. OLQ draws on the dictionary for the data descriptions.

ADS. ADS–ONLINE, the Application Development System On-Line, is a tool for developing simple query and update transactions without actual programming. Many query or update programs can be created merely by defining the positions of items on the screen. A simple language is provided for specifying data manipulations and calculations where needed.

ADS–BATCH, the Application Development System for batch programs, provides a similar vehicle for batch PROGRAM development. ADS–ONLINE and ADS–BATCH both make use of the data definitions contained in the dictionary.

ASF. The Automatic System Facility makes it possible to create highly standardized transactions and queries with virtually no programming. The user is, of course, limited to the predefined transactions and screen designs. Once again, the data definitions contained in the dictionary are utilized.

IDB. The Information Data Base provides a vehicle for storing data extracted from both IDMS data bases and conventional files. This data is stored in a form suitable for access via personal computers. IDB also uses the metadata stored in the dictionary.

GOLDENGATE. GOLDENGATE is personal computer software that can access the information Data Base. This product provides the typical features of an integrated personal computer software package. These include data base, spreadsheet, graphics, electronic mail, and document processing.

DDR. The Data Dictionary Reporter, is really IDMS Culprit in disguise. A comprehensive set of dictionary reports, written in Culprit, is provided. These may be modified by the user. Custom-designed reports can be written from scratch as well, but the user must understand the structure of the dictionary in order to take advantage of this feature.

Integration. Look at Figure 4.1 again. Notice that, as we've been mentioning, all of these system components reference data definitions stored in the Dictionary. These are placed in the Dictionary via Data Definition Language (DDL) statements and Data Dictionary Definition Language (DDDL) statements. Data Manipulation Language (DML) statements are interpreted by a precompiler which makes reference to the SCHEMA and SUBSCHEMA definitions stored in the Dictionary. Programs use data definitions extracted from the Dictionary. Culprit, OLQ, ADS, and other system components also refer to the SCHEMA and SUBSCHEMA definitions in the Dictionary. Formatting and validation definitions are extracted from the Dictionary as well. This means that the formatting and validation definitions must be in the Dictionary if the full power of the software is to be used effectively.

Once the SCHEMA and SUBSCHEMA definitions have been placed in the Dictionary, they are used by all system components. There is no need to rewrite them. This can result in consistent naming and reference if proper procedures are established and followed.

4.4 DICTIONARY CONTENT

As you can see, the IDMS Integrated Data Dictionary is the key component of the IDMS family of products. It contains Data Element definitions, Record and Set definitions, SCHEMA and SUBSCHEMA definitions, Data Media Control (DMCL) definitions, and also the teleprocessing network definition used by IDMS–DC. In the discussion that follows, we are going to deemphasize the things that are closely related to IDMS only and emphasize those that are common to all data dictionaries.

Figure 4.5 is an entity relationship diagram showing the basic types of information contained in this dictionary. This diagram follows the convention that an arrowhead indicates the many side of a one to many or many to many relationship. Cullinet documentation uses the word *entity* in the same way it is used in this book. It means an object or concept of interest. This entity relationship approach lends itself very handily to work with network data base management systems. Let's briefly review the entities and the relationships in which they can participate. Then we'll go back and look at each in more detail.

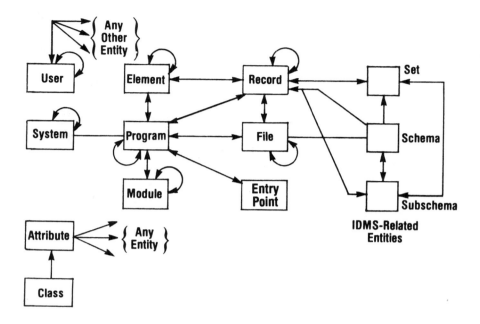

FIGURE 4.5   Basic IDD Entities and Relationships

USER. The USER entity is employed to store information about a USER of the data in the Data Base or a USER of the Dictionary. It is important to realize that there are, different types of USERs, and it can be important to keep track of the differences. This is discussed in more detail later in this chapter and also in Chapters 7, 8, and 10. This entity can be related to any of the others.

SYSTEM. The SYSTEM entity is used to store information about an application SYSTEM. A SYSTEM can have USERs, it can be related to other SYSTEMs, it can consist of SUBSYS-TEMs, and it can be related to its component PROGRAMs.

ELEMENT. The ELEMENT entity is used to store information about a data ELEMENT. ELEMENTs can have USERs.

Group ELEMENTs can be related to components. Occurrences of the same ELEMENT with different names can be classified as SYNONYMs. ELEMENTs can be related to PROGRAMs that manipulate them and to records that contain them.

PROGRAM. The PROGRAM entity is used to store information about a computer PROGRAM. PROGRAMs can have USERs. They can be related to other PROGRAMs and to SUBPROGRAMs and MODULEs. They can be related to SYSTEMs, RECORDs, ELEMENTs, FILEs and ENTRY POINTs.

MODULE. The MODULE entity is used to store information about a component of a computer PROGRAM. This might be a formal SUBPROGRAM, or it might just be a section of code. MODULEs can have USERs. They can be related to other MODULEs and also to PROGRAMs that contain or make use of them.

RECORD. The RECORD entity is used to store information about a Data Record contained in a File or Data Base. This could be a logical or conceptual Record as well as an actual physical Record. RECORDs can have USERs. They contain ELEMENTs. They can be related to PROGRAMs. They are contained in SCHEMA and SUBSCHEMAs. They can participate in SET relationships.

FILE. The FILE entity is used to store information about FILEs or collections of RECORDs. As is the case with RECORDs, FILEs can be logical or conceptual as well as physical. FILEs can have USERs. They consist of RECORDs. They can be related to PROGRAMs, to other FILEs, and to SCHEMAs.

ENTRY POINT. The ENTRY POINT entity is used to store information about a PROGRAM ENTRY POINT. An ENTRY POINT can have USERs.

SET, SCHEMA and SUBSCHEMA. These entities are some-what different from the entities described above. SET, SCHE-MA, and SUBSCHEMA are unique to CODASYL data bases.

The set entity is used to describe an IDMS SET relation-ship. SETs can be related to RECORDs, SCHEMAs, and SUBSCHEMAs.

The SCHEMA entity describes an IDMS SCHEMA. SCHEMAs can be related to SETs, RECORDs, FILEs, and SUBSCHEMAs.

The SUBSCHEMA entity describes an IDMS SUBSCHEMA. SUBSCHEMAs can be related to SCHEMAs, SETs, and RECORDs.

CLASS AND ATTRIBUTE. The CLASS and ATTRIBUTE entities need to be discussed together. Cullinet's Integrated Data Dictionary uses them to classify and categorize the other entities.

A CLASS is a category or type of entity. An ATTRIBUTE is a specific occurrence within a CLASS. The best way to under-stand this is through examples. Programming language can be considered a CLASS. COBOL, Fortran, Assembler, and the like can be considered ATTRIBUTEs within this CLASS, because they are specific programming languages. "Security Require-ment" can be considered a CLASS. "Secret," "Top Secret," "none," and so on can be considered ATTRIBUTEs within this CLASS because they are specific Security Requirements. CLASSes are related only to ATTRIBUTEs. ATTRIBUTEs are related to other entities. Thus, a specific PROGRAM might be related to the ATTRIBUTE COBOL within the CLASS PROGRAM-ING LANGUAGE. A specific FILE might be related to the ATTRIBUTE "Secret" within the CLASS "Security Requirement."

ATTRIBUTEs within a CLASS are used to classify or categorize other Dictionary Entities. The examples given in the preceding paragraph illustrate mechanisms that could then be used to retrieve the names of all COBOL PROGRAMs or all Top Secret FILEs. The CLASSes and ATTRIBUTEs we've just discussed are provided with the Dictionary by Cullinet. In addition, one can create installation-defined CLASSes and ATTRIBUTEs. Figure 4.6 illustrates a possible use of this facility. In this example, SYSA, SYSB, and so on are ATTRI-BUTEs within the CLASS "CPU and LOCATION." Some of the application SYSTEMs are run at all LOCATIONs. Others are run only at certain LOCATIONs.

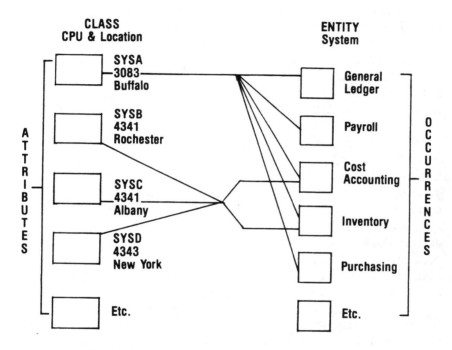

FIGURE 4.6   Class Attribute Example

Notice that in this context the word ATTRIBUTE is used the same way it is used in a discussion of entity relationship modelling. An ATTRIBUTE describes a feature or quality of some entity. In this situation, the ATTRIBUTE describes or classifies some dictionary entity. For example, COBOL PRO-GRAMMING LANGUAGE might be an ATTRIBUTE of PRO-GRAM PAY100. A CLASS is a family or category of values for a particular type of ATTRIBUTE.

4.5 DICTIONARY DATA BASE

As we've already noted, the IDMS Integrated Data Dictionary is actually an IDMS data base. Each of the entities and relationships is represented by one or more IDMS data Record types. There is a complex pattern of Record types and Set relationships.[2] Dictionary processing requires retrieval of specific RECORD occurrences based on specific relationships to other RECORD occurrences. For example, the dictionary satisfies a request to find out which PROGRAMs access a particular FILE by retrieving the RECORD occurrence that stands for the FILE and then traversing the appropriate SET occurrences to find RECORDs that represent the PROGRAMs.

The Dictionary Data Base is considerably more complex than the entity relationship diagram shown here, but we wouldn't benefit from going into more detail. We can obtain a better understanding by working with a higher level diagram. If you are involved in the physical implementation of this dictionary, you should refer to the vendor's documentation on this subject. You need to gain a detailed understanding of the actual Data Base network in order to create custom reports using the Data Dictionary Reporter, but you'll be better off if you make sure you understand the concepts discussed here before you get into that much detail.

The Cullinet Integrated Data Dictionary also contains a catalog of IDMS/R relational structures and the users who are authorized to access them. We will not cover that material here.

4.6 SYNONYMS AND VERSIONS

Before reviewing each of these Dictionary entities in more detail, we need to spend a little time on SYNONYMs and VERSIONs.

The IDMS Dictionary provides for multiple, numbered VERSIONs of Dictionary Entities. This facility might be used to keep a definition of the current or production VERSION of some dictionary entity in the same Dictionary with the definition of a new VERSION that is in use for development or testing. Keeping track of this sort of thing is a serious problem that arises in the maintenance of any complex system, whether or not a data base management system is in use. In a large shop, it is not unusual for two or more development teams to be working on different versions of something concurrently. Each team requires a unique data base and system definition and a unique test data base. If great care is not taken to keep track of the exact nature of each configuration and to plan implementation and conversion activities, a lot of trouble can result. As more and more organizations implement distributed data processing schemes, the problem of multiple data base system versions will become more common in production systems.

The need for synonyms arises when entity occurrences are known by multiple names. This may happen because different individuals have become accustomed to different terminologies or because there is some need for multiple names. The first of these two cases can be the most difficult to deal with. Because the basic concepts of data dictionary, data base, and data administration imply consistency and standardization, there is a strong temptation to insist on one and only one name for each entity type and occurrence. In practice, most of us will like this only if it means that others will change and begin using the names we like.

Naming standards and standard names can be one of the biggest sources of disagreement and debate in a data base or data dictionary project. This usually comes as a surprise to anyone who hasn't been through it before. We will discuss the subject in more detail in Chapters 7 and 8, but right now we'll just note that sometimes there is a good reason for multiple identifiers of the same thing. Sometimes synonyms are a necessity. The data element and record names used in programs are good examples of this. Different programming languages have different rules for naming things. Frequently, it isn't possible to use the typical COBOL data name in an assembly language program. While the converse may be possible, it isn't desirable.

The difference between a Cullinet VERSION and a SYNO-NYM is important. In the case of a version, there are actually two different objects that have the same name, as in the case of test and production versions. Two different record versions, each with a different configuration of elements, are an example. In the case of a synonym, there is one object with two names. For example, a specific element in a specific record might be called CUSTOMER–ACCOUNT–NUMBER in COBOL programs and CACCTNO in assembly language programs. It is important to note that these names are the ones used in programming. The actual names used by ordinary business people are usually hidden away in comment or description fields.

4.7 EXTENSIBILITY AND USER–DEFINED ENTITIES

As was noted in Chapter 3, contemporary data dictionaries provide a means for extending or customizing the dictionary data base. Cullinet's IDMS is no exception. The CLASS and ATTRIBUTE structure is one powerful technique. It can be used to categorize and classify the other Dictionary entities. The CLASS and ATTRIBUTE mechanism can also be used to create USER-defined entities. USER-defined nests are employed to define additional relationships. Nests are relationships between occurrences of the same entity type, such as PROGRAM to PROGRAM.

Keyword comments provide another form of extensibility. It is possible to create a special comments field with a user-assigned name. Maintenance, retrieval, and reporting can then be accomplished via the installation-defined keyword.

It is also possible to define named relationships between dictionary entities. These can then be maintained and reported by the installation-defined names.

4.8 MORE DETAILS ABOUT DICTIONARY CONTENT

This section of the chapter provides a more detailed discussion of each of the Dictionary entities. Our purpose is to clarify the types of information that can be stored in this, or any other, dictionary. The material does provide a useful overview for a user of the Cullinet dictionary, but it is not a substitute for the documentation and manuals provided with the software.

There are some descriptive attributes that are common to all entity types. These include PREPARED BY (which names the individual who created or entered the entity description), USER, ATTRIBUTE within CLASS, COMMENTS, and DEFINITION. COMMENTS and DEFINITION are discussed in detail in Chapters 7 and 8. Right now, just note that the prospective Dictionary user needs to stop and think about the types of information that need to be provided here and to establish standards to ensure consistency and readability.

USER. The USER entity is intended to stand for a USER of the Dictionary, of the data in a Data Base, of a SYSTEM, or of anything else that is documented in the Dictionary. It comes as a shock to most data processing personnel that it is not really clear who or what USERs are, and there can be more than one kind of USER. The standard IDMS Dictionary syntax provides for differentiation among USERs responsible for definition, USERs responsible for creation, USERs responsible for update, and USERs responsible for deletion of Dictionary entities. This means that a particular USER can be documented as having a particular responsibility regarding a particular Dictionary entity. Several things are important here.

These distinctions are designed to reflect responsibilities regarding Dictionary entity occurrences. The idea is that a specific individual or group is responsible for a specific RECORD or SYSTEM or PROGRAM definition as it appears in the Dictionary.

The different user categories are assigned via USER clauses, which are entered along with the specific entity definitions. They are not entered as a part of the USER entity definitions.

Different user categories have dictionary security implications. The dictionary software will allow only the USER who is responsible for definition to modify or delete the particular entity occurrence.

It is easy to confuse USERs of the Dictionary with users of systems, data, and others. This is an important distinction. It may also be important to distinguish between users and providers of data. This is discussed in more detail in Chapters 7 and 8.

The basic dictionary documentation doesn't provide a lot of guidance as to whether USERs are people, functions, departments, or some combination of these. It's up to you to decide. This is an issue that needs a lot of thought at the beginning of a Dictionary implementation project. It is very likely that additional types of USER entities will be required in a full Dictionary implementation. We will discuss this subject at greater length in Chapters 7 and 8.

The Dictionary syntax provides for a USER name, relationships to specific SYSTEMs, relationships to specific SUBSCHEMAs, relationships to other USERs, descriptive comments, and a number of IDMS-related capabilities, such as password. This book doesn't describe in great detail things that have meaning only in an IDMS operating environment.

The USER entity can be related to any other Dictionary entity via USER IS clauses associated with that entity.

SYSTEM and SUBSYSTEM. The SYSTEM and SUBSYSTEM are entities that are used to store information about an application SYSTEM. The standard syntax provides for NAME, VERSION, and the SYSTEM to SUBSYSTEM relationship. The SYSTEM or SUBSYSTEM to PROGRAM relationship is established via the syntax for adding PROGRAM entities to the dictionary. SYSTEMs can have USERs and ATTRIBUTEs.

ELEMENT. The ELEMENT entity is used to store information about a data element. The standard syntax provides for NAME, VERSION, validation criteria, physical description, and GROUP to SUBORDINATE ELEMENT relationships.

A great deal of confusion exists about the meaning of the word ELEMENT. Sometimes it is used to refer to an abstract concept such as a customer identifying number; sometimes it refers to a specific ELEMENT or field in a specific data record. There could be any number of fields which represent, or stand for, or contain an abstract element such as customer number. If you don't make this distinction and standardize the terminology used at your installation, you will find yourself involved in a lot of unnecessary arguments. Many dictionaries share the failure to make this distinction. We will address this subject again in Chapters 7, 8, and 11.

The following characteristics of ELEMENTs should also be noted:

ELEMENT to RECORD relationships are established via maintenance of the RECORD entity.

As noted previously, physical descriptions and validation criteria are particularly important if effective use is to be made of the Application Development System.

SYNONYMs and VERSIONs are also of particular concern when dealing with ELEMENTs.

ELEMENTs can have USERs and ATTRIBUTEs.

PROGRAM. The PROGRAM entity is used to store information about PROGRAMS. The standard syntax provides for NAME, VERSION, SYNONYM, descriptive information, and relationships to SYSTEM, RECORD, FILES, MODULE, SUBPROGRAM, AREA, SET, and SUBSCHEMA.

The relationships among PROGRAM and FILE, RECORD, SET, SUBPROGRAM, and MODULE deserve special attention. These can be created via the Data Dictionary Definition Language (DDDL) or they can be captured by the IDMS precompiler. The latter facility provides a way to capture these relationships more or less automatically. It is important to consider the impact of this feature on system performance. It is also extremely important to establish adequate controls over names and versions. If care is not taken, things can get out of hand quickly.

PROGRAMs can have USERs and ATTRIBUTEs.

MODULE. The MODULE entity is used to store information about a component of a PROGRAM. The standard syntax provides for a NAME, VERSION, and relationships to SYSTEM and SUBSYSTEM.

This dictionary also provides the ability to store MODULE source code. When this is done, the IDMS precompiler will, on command, copy the MODULE into a source program and will record MODULE to PROGRAM relationships as this takes place.

MODULEs can have USERs and ATTRIBUTEs.

RECORD. The RECORD entity is used to store information about Data Records. REPORTs and TRANSACTIONs are really special kinds of RECORDs. This dictionary allows them to be used as keywords which create specially identified occurrences of the RECORD entity.

RECORDs can have NAMEs, VERSIONs, SYNONYMs, relationships to FILEs, and component ELEMENTs.

The physical characteristics of ELEMENTs included in a RECORD can be the same as those contained in the ELEMENT entity definitions, or they can be uniquely defined for the particular RECORD definition.

PROGRAM to RECORD relationships can be incorporated in the appropriate PROGRAM entity definitions, or they can be established when the precompiler copies a RECORD into a PROGRAM. This technique provides a powerful means for ensuring that all programs use standard RECORD definitions and ELEMENT names and that all PROGRAM to RECORD relationships are recorded. If this technique is adopted, careful control of NAMEs and VERSIONs is essential. There are also some system performance considerations, since all program compilations will update the Dictionary Data Base.

RECORDs can have USERs and ATTRIBUTEs. They can be included in SCHEMAs and SUBSCHEMAs and can participate in SET relationships.

FILE. The FILE entity is used to store information about a FILE. FILEs can have NAMEs, VERSIONs, USERs, and descriptions. They can be related to RECORDs and to other FILEs, as well as to PROGRAMs. The FILE to PROGRAM relationship is established via maintenance of the PROGRAM entity.

FILEs can have USERs and ATTRIBUTEs.

ENTRY POINT. The ENTRY POINT entity is used to store information regarding a PROGRAM ENTRY POINT. ENTRY POINTs have NAMEs and descriptions, as well as relationships to PROGRAMs. These relationships are established via maintenance of the program entity.

ENTRY POINTs can have USERs and ATTRIBUTEs.

SET, SCHEMA, and SUBSCHEMA. SET, SCHEMA, and SUBSCHEMA are IDMS-related entities. They are usually created, defined, and maintained in a manner different from the other entities. Since their nature and use are very specific to IDMS or CODASYL systems, they will not be dealt with in any detail here.

CLASS and ATTRIBUTE. These are two entities that have been described in detail in section 4.4. They have NAMEs and descriptions. CLASS can be related only to ATTRIBUTE. ATTRIBUTE can be related to any other entity. These relationships are established via maintenance of the subject entity.

Other Entities. A number of additional dictionary entities are related to various Cullinet software products or features. These include MESSAGE, PANEL, MAP, TASK, QUEUE, DESTINATION, LINE, TERMINAL, and TABLE. These will not be discussed here.

4.9 SOURCES OF DATA

The active nature of this dictionary can lead to some confusion regarding data sources and maintenance techniques. Much of the data can be entered only via the Data Dictionary Definition Language (DDDL). This is particularly true for descriptive information and for entities, such as USER, that are not strictly parts of the Cullinet software. This approach to maintenance presupposes someone who decides how the dictionary will be used, establishes standards, and possibly does all the updating as well. Depending on the nature of the organization, this might be one person or a sizable group. The job title might be data base administrator, data administrator, data dictionary administrator, librarian, or what have you. It is essential that some one person or group be given this responsibility.

Some of the data is generated as a by-product of designing and implementing an IDMS data base. The Data Definition Language (DDL) can be used for this purpose. SCHEMA, SUBSCHEMA, and SET definitions are of this nature. RECORDs and ELEMENTs can be maintained via DDDL or DDL. Some of the more descriptive data about these can be entered only via DDDL. Usually, either a data base administrator or a system development group performs this maintenance.

Some data can be captured automatically via the IDMS precompiler. The precompiler will process programs that use conventional files as well as those that access IDMS data bases. This can be a great labor-saving device and can also ensure that dictionary content is accurate, consistent, and up-to-date—but, it is a mixed blessing. There can be significant system performance considerations, especially in a large shop. Furthermore, if PROGRAM, MODULE, FILE, and RECORD names are not standardized, the dictionary can be filled with unusable and even meaningless entries. The results of uncontrolled use of this feature could be a big surprise.

Data about FILEs, RECORDs and ELEMENTs, can also be captured via a syntax converter and dictionary loader system that analyzes existing COBOL programs and creates dictionary updates. The quality of information obtained in this way is highly dependent on the quality and consistency of RECORD and ELEMENT names that have been used in the programs. In many installations, this approach will require a lengthy review, edit, and scrub procedure. This will be discussed in more detail in Chapter 11.

When multiple sources of data exist, the IDMS dictionary provides "BUILDER CODES" that indicate the source from which a particular data item was obtained.

4.10 CONCLUDING REMARKS

Some of the preceding might seem to be of interest only to a user of this particular dictionary, but that isn't really the case. Possibly an active system like this one offers more opportunity for confusion, but the sources and reliability of the data placed in the dictionary become an important issue in any dictionary implementation. This subject will be addressed again in Chapters 7 and 8.

This dictionary also provides for the existence of multiple dictionary occurrences. This is becoming more important as organizations move to multiple CPU and multiple location environments. We will discuss this issue in more detail in Chapters 8, 10, and 11.

NOTES

1. *Logical* is another of those words that must be evaluated in context and with great care. Here, it means a pseudo-record

that doesn't really exist in the physical data base. VIEW is another term for this. The word *view* is generally encountered in a relational environment. In a different context, *logical data base* refers to a design that captures the essence or logic of the problem without reference to a physical implementation. In this context, a logical record is merely a collection of fields or elements that seem to go together and may or may not be stored together. In an IMS environment, a logical relationship is one that provides an alternative way of viewing the data.

2. There is an IDMS SCHEMA which defines the Dictionary Data Base. This SCHEMA must be defined in the dictionary along with any others. This is a source of confusion if it is not understood.

References

Association for Computing Machinery. *CODASYL Data Base Task Group Report.* New York: Association for Computing Machinery, April 1971.

Cullinet Software, Inc. *Integrated Data Dictionary: Summary Description.* Westwood, Mass.: Cullinet Software, Inc., 1984.

———*Integrated Data Dictionary: Features Guide.* Westwood, Mass.: Cullinet Software, Inc., 1984.

———*Integrated Data Dictionary: User's Guide.* Westwood, Mass.: Cullinet Software, Inc., 1984.

H. Lefkovits, E. Sibley, and S. Lefkovitz. *Information Resource/ Data Dictionary Systems.* Wellesley, Mass.: QED Information Sciences, Inc., 1983, ch. 5.

5 The IBM DB/DC Data Dictionary

This chapter discusses IBM's DB/DC Data Dictionary. Words such as PROGRAM are capitalized when they are used in the context of IMS or Dictionary keywords. They are not capitalized when they are used in a more ordinary sense.

5.1 AN IMPORTANT WARNING

This chapter illustrates some features of data dictionaries by discussing the IBM product. It contains material on the philosophy, features, and use of the DB/DC Data Dictionary. It is not a substitute for a careful reading of the technical manuals provided by the vendor. New versions of this software are always under development and there is no way to guarantee that the version that is current when you read this book will not be significantly different from the version that was current when the book was written. Also, since the intent is to illustrate dictionary features and their use rather than to provide a definitive reference for a particular product, details are sometimes omitted. Emphasis is placed on the logic of the system rather than on the technical detail. A data dictionary is a complex system. Technical system details are important, but it is very easy to get lost in the technical details and forget what the system and processing are really about.

It is assumed that the reader is familiar with the content of Chapter 4. Some of the same things must be repeated, but wherever it is possible, concepts that have already been presented there are not presented in detail here.

Be sure to read the vendor's technical manuals thoroughly and attend appropriate training classes before attempting to use the IBM Dictionary. Implementing and using a product of this complexity is not a trivial task.

5.2 THE DB/DC DATA DICTIONARY

Depending on your point of view, the IBM Dictionary is either a *passive* dictionary or a hybrid *active/passive* dictionary. You can run the related data base management system, IMS, without the Dictionary. The converse, however, is not true; you must install IMS to use the IBM Dictionary. There is provision for using the Dictionary to generate the data base definitions used by IMS. There is also a precompiler that will copy definitions from the Dictionary into programs. The evolution and development of this dictionary has been parallel with, and somewhat independent of that of IMS. In recent years, IBM has realized the benefits to be derived from the use of an active dictionary and has added many active features to this dictionary.

5.3 INFORMATION MANAGEMENT SYSTEM

Because the dictionary does make use of and interact with IMS, a few words of description are necessary. IMS, the

Information Management System, has been IBM's premier large-scale data base management system for years. It is an extremely powerful and complex designer-oriented data base management system. That is, it is intended for use by systems development professionals who are prepared to spend significant amounts of time in highly structured design and implementation activities. The flexibility and power of the system can present many pitfalls for the unwary or casual user. IMS error recovery and restart facilities are unparalleled.

IMS uses a hierarchical data structure. Data elements or fields are organized into *segments*. IMS segments are processed more or less the way records are processed in other systems. Segment types are organized into hierarchical structures with root or parent segments and dependent or child segments. A root may have many dependents. In the pure hierarchical structure a dependent may be associated with but one root or parent. IMS circumvents this limitation by providing for the definition of alternative hierarchies, which are called logical data bases.[1] Thus, a particular segment may be the root in one definition and the dependent in another. The system resolves this via an elaborate indexing technique. As a general rule, only the data base administrator need be deeply concerned with this issue.

The segments are organized into physical records in a manner appropriate to the hierarchical data structure. Each set of records is, in IMS terminology, a separate data base. Thus, while the system designers or users may think of one data base, the data base administrator is likely to talk about several physical IMS data bases. Separate program views of the data are provided. The concept is similar to the CODASYL SCHEMA/SUBSCHEMA concept, but these terms are not normally used. The view of a segment given to a particular program is not necessarily identical with the actual segment in the data base.

The IMS command and definition languages tend to be oriented toward programming technicians. They are considered formidable and arcane by some, because of the somewhat forbidding format. In fact, as data manipulation languages go, the IMS language, DL/I, is relatively straightforward and easy to use.

IMS has many devoted adherents and many dedicated critics. It is widely used. The future of IMS may be clouded by IBM's recent introduction of relational data base management systems. However, IBM and many IBM customers have so much invested in IMS-based systems that IMS is likely to be with us for many more years. The question is of interest here mainly because, at this time, it is necessary to establish the minimum IMS environment in order to operate the DB/DC Data Dictionary and because the Dictionary does provide for IMS definitions.

5.4   OTHER PRODUCTS

The IBM DB/DC Data Dictionary does interact with several other IBM products: GIS/VS, IMSADF, DMS/CICS/VS, SDF/CICS, and Database2.

The GIS/VS Query language can be used to obtain some dictionary reports. IMSADF, DMS/CICS/VS, and SDF/CICS are essentially systems for generating screens and transactions. Source statements used by each can be stored in the dictionary.

5.5   DATABASE2

Database2 is IBM's relational data base management system for large-scale mainframe systems. SQL/DS is a similar product intended for the IBM DOS/VS operating system environment.

At the time this is being written, utility programs exist that will utilize the content of the Data Dictionary in the process of creating relational databases from IMS data bases or conventional files. IBM has also announced development of dictionary facilities for recording descriptions of relational databases.

Database2 has its own CATALOG, which contains definitions of the relational databases and their users, but at this time there is no direct connection between Database2 and the DB/DC Data Dictionary. By the time you read this, this issue may have been resolved.

5.6 DICTIONARY CONTENT

The content of the DB/DC Dictionary is defined in terms of SUBJECTs, CATEGORies, and RELATIONSHIPs. A SUBJECT is really an entity occurrence in disguise. It is a particular object, real or abstract. Examples are the program called PAY100 and the element called EMPNO. A CATEGORY is really an entity type, such as PROGRAM or ELEMENT. A RELATION-SHIP type may be defined between two CATEGORIES. A RELATIONSHIP occurrence for a collection of these, such as all the elements and segments that constitute a particular data base, is referred to as a STRUCTURE. The Dictionary provides commands and operators that manipulate SUBJECTs and RELATIONSHIPs, and commands and operators that manipulate entire STRUCTUREs. SUBJECTs must be related in accordance with the hierarchical structure illustrated in Figure 5.1. That is, those shown near the top of the diagram must be in place before those near the bottom can be added. The rules for deleting and copying STRUCTUREs are also based on this hierarchy. These rules are fairly complex and require careful study. We will not deal with them here.

Let's briefly review the standard CATEGORies. Then, we'll go over each in more detail.

SYSTEM is used to represent a major application system, such as Accounts Payable.

JOB refers to a collection of programs treated as a single unit of work. It is a common practice to group a series of programs into a single job for operational simplicity.

PROGRAM is used to represent an individual program or job step.

MODULE refers to a component of a program.

SYSDEF defines an IMS operating configuration.

TRANSACTION is used to describe a specific transaction or request type to be processed by a system or program. "Add Customer Account" would be an example.

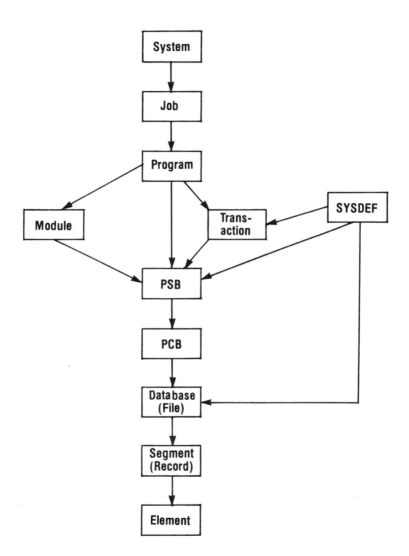

FIGURE 5.1   Hierarchy of DB/DC Subjects

PSB and *PCB* stand for Program Specification Block and Program Communications Block. They define the data base views for specific programs. They are similar in concept to CODASYL SUBSCHEMAs.

DATABASE refers to an IMS data base. This CATEGORY is also used to represent a conventional file.

SEGMENT refers to an IMS segment. This CATEGORY is also used to represent a conventional record.

ELEMENT is used to describe an individual data element or field.

There are several additional CATEGORies that are not incorporated in this hierarchy.

DDUSER is used to represent dictionary users.

CATEGORY is used to represent an installation-defined CATEGORY.

RELTYPE is used to represent an installation-defined RELATIONSHIP type.

STRTYPE is used to define an installation-defined STRUCTURE type.

5.7 MORE DETAILS ABOUT DICTIONARY CONTENT

All Dictionary categories or subject definitions share a number of common descriptor or attribute types. These are NAME, SUBJECT DATA, and RELATIONSHIPS.

All CATEGORies provide for DESCRIPTION and USER DATA. There is one DESCRIPTION group. There are five USER DATA groups. Each group consists of up to 255 lines of text. Each line is numbered.

A DB/DC SUBJECT *NAME* consists of four components, separated by commas. The first is a STATUS code. Valid STATUS codes are P for Production, T for Test, and 0 through 9 for additional test versions. Some of the rules for combining subjects into structures depend on the STATUS codes. An entire structure may contain, at most, two STATUS codes. If there are two, one of the two must be Production. Subjects with Production STATUS may own only other subjects with the same STATUS. Subjects with Test STATUS may own others with Production STATUS. While this appears unduly complex at first glance, it is actually quite reasonable. Systems, programs, and data bases normally migrate from Test to Production status. Test versions often contain many of the same components as production versions. The migration from Test to Production must be carefully controlled.

The next component of a NAME is ENTITY TYPE, which is sometimes referred to as SUBJECT CODE. It is a one-character code that clarifies the nature of the subject. DATABASE subjects may be categorized as conventional files or as one of several types of IMS Database or Index. SEGMENTS may be classified as records or IMS segments. SEGMENTS and ELEMENTS are also classified according to the programming languages used to manipulate them.

The next component of a NAME is USER NAME, which can have up to 31 characters. This is what we might tend to think of as the actual name. However, we have to be careful. These are normally data-processing-oriented or programmer-oriented names, which may have little meaning to accountants, salespeople, bankers, or users in general. The ''real'' name which has a business meaning will appear among the descriptive comments. This is true of most dictionaries—and it is the source of a lot of confusion.

The final component of a NAME is an OCCURRENCE NUMBER. This is a number from 0 to 255 which is used to distinguish between subjects that otherwise would have the same name. We might best think of a combination of STATUS and OCCURRENCE as equivalent to the Cullinet VERSION.

Some of the subjects (ELEMENT, SEGMENT, DATABASE, PCB, and user-defined) can have alternate NAMEs, called ALIASes. They are similar to the SYNONYMs provided in the Cullinet dictionary.

SUBJECT DATA consists of attributes, descriptions, user data, and IMS-oriented data. ATTRIBUTES are predefined data items. These vary from category to category. DESCRIPTION and USER DATA are free-form text. The IMS data doesn't really interest us here.

RELATIONSHIPS are connections between subjects. Some RELATIONSHIPs may have data; others may not. Refer to Figure 5.2 for an entity relationship diagram which illustrates the standard Dictionary categories and relationships. Each is now discussed in turn.

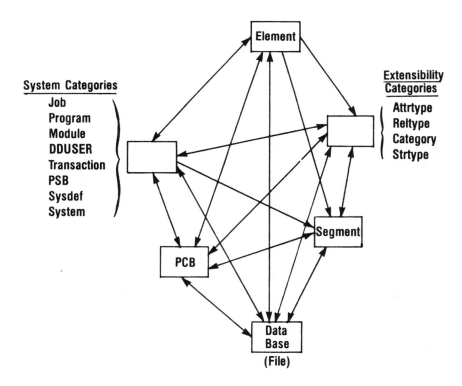

FIGURE 5.2 DB/DC Categories and Relationships

The *DATABASE* category stands for an IMS data base or a conventional file. A detailed physical description is provided. There is also provision for Descriptive and User Data text. A DATABASE may be related to another DATABASE to an ELEMENT, to a PCB, to a SYSTEM, or to a SEGMENT.

The *SEGMENT* category stands for an IMS segment or a record in a conventional file. There is provision for a detailed physical description, as well as Descriptive and User Data text. A SEGMENT may be related to other SEGMENTs, DATABASEs, PCBs, SYSTEMs, or ELEMENTs.

The *ELEMENT* category stands for a data element or field. There is provision for physical description, as well as Descriptive and User Data text. An ELEMENT may be related to other ELEMENTs, DATABASEs, PCBs, SYSTEMs, or SEGMENTs.

A *PCB* is an IMS Program Communication Block. This defines a view of an IMS data base held by a particular program or user. It is roughly equivalent to a CODASYL SUBSCHEMA. A PCB may be related to other PCBs, ELEMENTs, DATABASEs, SYSTEMs, or SEGMENTs.

SYSTEM is actually a family of categories. A SYSTEM SUBJECT may represent a SYSTEM, a JOB, a PROGRAM, a MODULE, a TRANSACTION, a DDUSER, a SYSDEF, or a PSB (Program Specification Block). A SYSTEM is a complete data processing system such as Inventory or Payroll. A JOB is a collection of programs, treated as a unit for operating efficiency. A PROGRAM is a single computer program. A MODULE is a component of a PROGRAM. A TRANSACTION is a unit of work performed by a PROGRAM, such as a balance inquiry. A DDUSER is a user of the dictionary. A SYSDEF is an IMS-oriented system definition. A PSB is an IMS data base definition built into a program. Each of the SYSTEM categories provides for appropriate physical attributes, plus Description and User Data text. Any SYSTEM subject may be related to any other and also to a DATABASE, a SEGMENT, a PCB, or an ELEMENT. Subjects in the SYSTEM categories may not have ALIASes.

The RELATIONSHIPS that may contain data are DATABASE with SEGMENT, PCB with SEGMENT, SEGMENT with ELEMENT, ELEMENT with ELEMENT, SYSDEF with DATABASE, SYSDEF with PSB, SYSDEF with TRANSACTION, and PSB with TRANSACTION.

Extensibility Categories. Four extensibility categories are provided. These are employed to construct user-defined CATEGORIES, RELATIONSHIPS, ATTRIBUTES, and STRUCTURES.

1. The ATTRTYPE category is used to define new attributes or descriptors, which may then be associated with other categories or relationships.

2. The CATEGORY category is used to define new categories or subject types.

3. The RELTYPE category is used to define new relationships between installation-defined categories or between installation-defined categories and standard categories. These installation-defined relationships can have descriptive names. One can define forward and reverse names. For example, DDUSER MAINTAINS PROGRAM and PROGRAM MAINTAINED BY DDUSER would be names for the same relationship. Installation-defined relationship types can also have attributes.

4. The STRTYPE category is used to define new structures.

Possible uses for these extensibility categories are virtually unlimited. Some of the potential is indicated in Chapters 7, 8, and 10.

5.8 SOURCES OF DATA

As is the case with the Cullinet dictionary (and with other dictionaries as well), subject definitions may be entered directly through dictionary commands, some definitions may be obtained by scanning source code or program copy libraries, and there is a precompiler that will copy data definitions from the dictionary into programs. This dictionary does not have extensive facilities for automatic capture of relationships.

5.9 REPORTING

The DB/DC dictionary provides extensive reporting capabilities, as well as on-line inquiry and update facilities. A Program Access Facility (PAF) provides for implementation of custom-designed reports.

NOTES

1. As discussed in note 2. for Chapter 4, *logical* has a special meaning here.

References

H. Lefkovits, E. Sibley, and S. Lefkovits, *Information Resource/ Data Dictionary Systems* (Wellesley, Mass.: QED Information Sciences, Inc., 1983), Ch. 3; and three reference manuals from IBM Corporation: *OS/VS DB/DC Data Dictionary: General Information Manual* (San Jose, Calif.: IBM Corp., 1983); *DB/DC Data Dictionary: User's Guide* (San Jose, Calif.: IBM Corp., 1977); and *DB/DC Data Dictionary: Applications Guide* (San Jose, Calif.: IBM Corp., 1979).

6 DATAMANAGER

This chapter discusses Manager Software Products' DATA-MANAGER. As in Chapters 4 and 5, words such as PROGRAM are capitalized when they are used in the context of Dictionary keywords. They are not capitalized when they are used in a more ordinary sense.

6.1 AN IMPORTANT WARNING

This chapter illustrates some things about data dictionaries by discussing the MSP product. It contains material on the philosophy, features, and use of DATAMANAGER. It is not a substitute for a careful reading of the technical manuals provided by the vendor. New versions of this software are always under development. There is no way to guarantee that the version which is current when you read this book is not significantly different from the version which was current when the book was written. Also, since the intent is to illustrate dictionary features and their use rather than to provide a definitive reference for a particular product, details are sometimes omitted. Emphasis is placed on the logic of the system as opposed to technical detail. A Data Dictionary is a complex system. Technical system details are important. However, it is very easy to get lost in the technical details and forget what the system and processing are really about.

Also, it is assumed that the reader is familiar with the content of Chapters 4 and 5. Some of the same things must be repeated. But, wherever it is possible, concepts which have already been presented there are not elaborated on here.

Be sure to read the vendor's technical manuals thoroughly and attend appropriate training classes before attempting to use DATAMANAGER. Implementing a product of this complexity is not a trivial task.

6.2 DATAMANAGER

DATAMANAGER is an example of a data dictionary that does not depend on any data base management system. As such, it is classified as a *passive* dictionary. As is the case with the IBM DB/DC Dictionary, DATAMANAGER can be used to generate the data base definitions used by a DBMS and also to generate source language program statements. ''Selectable'' units are available which allow DATAMANAGER to interface with a number of data base management systems, including ADABAS, IDMS, IMS, SYSTEM 2000, and TOTAL.

The selectable unit concept is an important feature of DATAMANAGER. One can purchase only those components needed at a particular installation. The basic system components are contained in the nucleus. Selectable units include the aforementioned DBMS support units, units that allow access to the dictionary via commonly used telecommunications monitors, units that generate source language statements for various programming systems, security facilities, and extensibility or user-defined syntax unit, a user-defined output unit, and others.

6.3 OTHER MANAGER PRODUCTS

Manager Software Products also markets CONTROLMANA-
GER, DESIGNMANAGER, SOURCEMANAGER, PROJECTMAN-
AGER, and TESTMANAGER. These form an integrated family
of products which utilize the DATAMANAGER dictionary data
base as a central data resource.

CONTROLMANAGER provides a standardized user interface
for the entire MANAGER product line. Features include
maintenance of user profiles, user-defined syntax, user-
defined input and output formats, and an on-line HELP
facility.

DESIGNMANAGER is an automated data base design and
data-modelling tool. It can be used for logical data base design
and also for enterprise modelling.

SOURCEMANAGER is a comprehensive source library and
application development system. It provides for the implementation of reusable code and for automated program generation.
It can also be used to check program source code for conformity
to installation standards.

PROJECTMANAGER is a project resource management and
budget control system.

TESTMANAGER provides an environment for generation of
test data and management of program testing.

6.4 DICTIONARY CONTENT

The DATAMANAGER dictionary data base consists of information about MEMBERS. A DATAMANAGER MEMBER is

equivalent to an Integrated Data Dictionary ENTITY or a DB/DC Dictionary CATEGORY. We've noted before that there is very little standardization of terminology in the data processing world.

6.4.1   Common Elements

In general, any MEMBER can have a NAME, an ALIAS, a DESCRIPTION, a USERNAME or OWNER, a STATUS, VERSIONs, SECURITY, CATALOGUEs, and EFFECTIVE and OBSOLETE DATEs, as well as some other descriptors that are not relevant here. You should be able to note that these are by and large similar to those discussed in Chapters 4 and 5.

NAME. MEMBER NAMEs can be up to 32 characters long. These provide the primary key for storing, retrieving, and updating MEMBERs. Synonyms can be dealt with by specifying additional names for MEMBERs.

ALIAS. An ALIAS provides for an alternative name. It can have up to 79 characters. ALIASes might provide for end user names or they might provide appropriate names for use with various programming languages. MSP documentation states that an ALIAS is an alternative NAME required for technical reasons.

DESCRIPTION. DESCRIPTIONs provide for a text description of MEMBERs. There is no practical limit to the number of characters.

USERNAME or OWNER. If the security module is installed, registered USERs of the dictionary can be designated as OWNERs of dictionary data. As such, they control updating of the data.

STATUS. If the STATUS module is installed, up to 255 distinct STATUSes can be used to identify different views or versions of dictionary data. This feature has the effect of providing subdictionaries or logical dictionaries. It can be used for keeping a historical record of obsolete versions of things or for segregating test from production.

VERSION. VERSION can be used to identify up to 15 distinct VERSIONs of a MEMBER.

SECURITY–CLASSIFICATION and ACCESS–AUTHORITY. SECURITY–CLASSIFICATION provides for a description of data security requirements. It can be up to 256 characters long. ACCESS–AUTHORITY identifies those who are authorized to use the data and tells whether the authorization allows reading, updated, or security control.

    Both of these clauses refer to the enterprise data described in the dictionary. As noted above access to dictionary data is controlled via the security module.

CATALOGUE. CATALOGUE entries provide a means for creating a cross-reference to MEMBERs with similar uses or characteristics. A particular CATALOGUE entry may consist of up to 79 characters. The same CATALOGUE identifier may be assigned to any number of MEMBERs. There is no practical limit to the number of classifications which can be assigned to a given MEMBER.

EFFECTIVE–DATE and OBSOLETE–DATE. These descriptors provide a means of recording and controlling the effective or useful life of a MEMBER or a VERSION of a MEMBER.

6.4.2 MEMBER Types

The standard MEMBER types are ITEM, GROUP or ARRAY,

FILE, DATABASE, MODULE, PROGRAM, and SYSTEM. Figure 6.1 illustrates the standard relationships that are provided. As we discuss each MEMBER in turn, you should be able to note that they are very similar to the ENTITies and CATEGORies discussed in the preceding two chapters. Each of these can be assigned many more descriptors than are discussed here. The discussion is intended merely to convey the general nature of DATAMANAGER. You'll have to refer to the vendor's documentation for more detail.

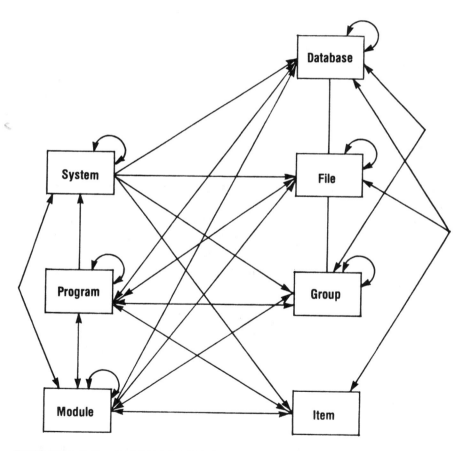

FIGURE 6.1   DATAMANAGER Entities and Relationships

ITEM. An ITEM represents our old friend, the data element. DATAMANAGER provides for those descriptors we've already discussed and also for a complete physical description of each ITEM.

GROUP or ARRAY. A GROUP or ARRAY is a collection of ITEMs for some reason can be dealt with as a unit. In addition to the descriptors we have already discussed, DATAMANAGER provides for specification of the component ITEMs or GROUPs or ARRAYs. In DATAMANAGER, a record is entered as a GROUP. You might want to use a CATALOGUE entry to identify MEMBERs that represent record types. A separate MEMBER type is not provided.

FILE. A FILE is a collection of records. Provision is made for the common descriptors and also for specification of the appropriate record types. Provision is made for specifying the physical characteristics of the FILE.

DATABASE. DATABASE MEMBERS will occur only if one or more DBMS interface units have been selected. These will then be appropriate for and specific to a particular DBMS.

MODULE. A MODULE is a unit of PROGRAM code. Provision is made for relating MODULEs to data acted on, to other MODULEs, and to PROGRAMs.

PROGRAM. This MEMBER can be used to represent PRO-GRAMs and SUBPROGRAMs. A program can be related to the data it acts on, to other PROGRAMS, and to MODULEs.

SYSTEM. A SYSTEM is a collection of PROGRAMs. SYSTEMs can be related to PROGRAMs, DATABASEs, FILEs, RECORDs, GROUPs, and ITEMs.

6.5   USER–DEFINED SYNTAX

The USER DEFINED SYNTAX selectable unit provides extensibility. The user can create new entity types, relationships, and descriptors or attributes. As is the case with other complete dictionaries, your ingenuity and inventiveness are the only limitations to what can be accomplished. Just about any type of metadata can be described to and stored in the DATAMANAGER data dictionary.

6.6   SUMMARY

We've already noted that DATAMANAGER is included to provide an example of a dictionary that does not depend on any specific DBMS. The features and facilities are generally comparable to the other dictionaries which we've discussed. The vendor has also made an effort to provide, via selectable units, dictionary entities that can model all of the leading data base management systems. This dictionary is, of necessity, more *passive* than dictionaries that are integrated with data base management systems.

References

Management Systems and Programming, Inc. *DATAMANAGER Fact Book* (1980)
———. *DATAMANAGER Release 5.0 Announcement* (1983).
———. *DATAMANAGER User's Guide* (1983).
———. *How to Get Started* (1983).

All of the above are published by, and can be obtained from, Management Systems and Programming, Inc., 131 Hartwell Ave., Lexington, MA 02173-3126, USA or Management Systems and Programming, Ltd., 71 Gloucester Place, London W1H 3PF, United Kingdom.

7 A Simple Dictionary Implementation

So far, we've reviewed the features and content of dictionaries in general and amplified the concepts by looking at three specific products. Now let's take a look at a possible dictionary implementation. First, we'll do some analysis and design. Then we'll look at implementations of our design using two of the dictionaries that we've become familiar with. This chapter has an informal narrative format. Issues are dealt with more or less as they arise. The same issues are reviewed more formally in Chapter 8. This review may cause us to revise some of our earlier, more naive ideas.

It is important for you to realize that the recommendations and suggestions given here are just that—recommendations and suggestions. You are going to have to evaluate your particular situation and decide whether or not they will work in your environment. The approach and methodology are more important than the specific details of either dictionary implementation.

7.1   THE NEED FOR DESIGN

It should be clear from the last three chapters that implementing a data dictionary is not a process in which you can select a package, install it on your system, and start using it. You should view the software you receive from the vendor as a sort of *do-it-yourself dictionary kit*. So many features and options are available in a contemporary dictionary that analysis and design steps are an essential preliminary.[1]

The material in this chapter covers many of the issues that need attention. If there is any error in the number of issues raised, it is one of omission. You will see that, without a doubt, the implementation of a dictionary is not something to be undertaken casually.

7.2   OBJECTIVES

A good way to start any system design activity is to set some objectives. We will discuss this at greater length in Chapters 10 and 11. For now, let's say we are going to install a dictionary in order to keep track of systems, jobs, programs, and files or data bases. In other words, the goal is to accomplish the housekeeping within a systems development department. The systems development department and possibly the computer operations department will be the users of the dictionary. The dictionary data base and reporting structure will be designed to fulfill their needs and make their jobs easier. Let's further assume that we've devoted the necessary time to a study of our data processing operation and the problems we have and have developed a list of specific objectives. These are listed below.

Standardize the names, definitions, and physical descriptions of the data elements used in all programs. Standardize the column headings used on reports and the labels used on display formats.

Document which data is kept in which files or databases or schemas.

Document which programs, jobs, and systems access and update which data elements in which files or databases or schemas.

Document which reports and screens are produced by which programs, jobs, and systems.

Document which modules and subprograms are included in which programs.

Document processing schedules, file back-up and retention, and responsibilities for program and jobstream maintenance.

These objectives seem limited enough, particularly in light of claims that are made regarding the things that can be accomplished with a data dictionary. Even so, we need to determine whether these objectives are appropriate to our situation. Both the objectives and their susceptibility to achievement imply a number of assumptions.

7.3   ASSUMPTIONS

So, before we start, we'd better take a little time to examine the assumptions that provide the basis for these objectives.

A data base administration or data dictionary administration group exists and has been formally charged with installing and maintaining a data dictionary.

Our data processing shop has expressed the desire and willingness to standardize naming conventions and procedures. We won't let all the procedures be bypassed the first time there is a rush project. (It is highly likely, especially in a larger organization, that design teams will state that adhering to standard procedures will slow them down and delay completion of critical projects. Sometimes the delay is an illusion. Sometimes it is real.) It is usually very expensive, if not impossible, to go back and fix things up when standard procedures have been bypassed. There must be commitment to a managed and controlled approach to data processing. Managers and workers must share this commitment.

It will be possible to obtain good data element, transaction, and system definitions for new and existing systems. When the same data element appears in several files, disguised as several different fields with different names, we will be able to recognize it. *This is a big assumption.*

We have, or can obtain, good documentation of our existing data elements, files, modules, subprograms, programs, copy libraries, load libraries, job control language files, systems, and so on. Many methods that have been proposed for implementing data dictionaries and data bases seem to assume that one starts with a clean slate and doesn't have to worry about existing systems. We might have to do a lot of preliminary housekeeping before we can get started.

We have a well-defined concept of what a system is. We know which systems we have. This is not as silly as it sounds. Some large organizations really don't have clear, consistent documentation showing what systems they have and who the users of each are.

We are not doing data administration for the entire organization right now. We are just getting our own data processing house in order.

The validity of assumptions like these must be carefully examined before any data dictionary project is begun.

7.4 DATA MODEL

Our next steps involve designing a data base to contain the information. Since we believe in an organized approach to things, we'll start with an entity relationship diagram (or, if you prefer, a logical data model, or if you come from a slightly different school, a conceptual data model).

Whatever we decide to call this, it is illustrated in Figure 7.1. This diagram uses the convention that a single arrow represents the "many" side of a one to many or many to many relationship. Let's discuss each entity and relationship in turn.

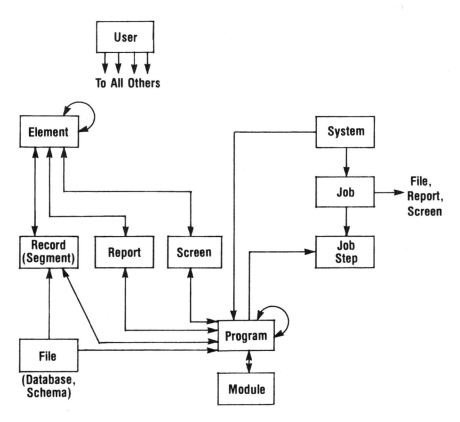

FIGURE 7.1   Conceptual Model of a Simple Dictionary

USER. This entity represents a USER of the dictionary, more or less. Specifically, this entity will stand for an individual responsible for some of the dictionary content. USERs will have names and descriptive information. It will be possible to relate a USER to any other dictionary entity.

ELEMENT. This entity represents the smallest unit of data. Most of our programmers and analysts use the word *field.* We think these mean the same thing.

We believe that each element should have a single standard name and definition. We realize that there may be several different fields in several different records in several different files (or DATABASEs or SCHEMAs) that represent the same data. For example, a part number appears in an inventory record, in a shop order record, in a purchase order record, in an inspection record, and in others as well. But, we don't think this is a problem. If it's a part number, it's a part number. All of our programs are written in COBOL. They should all refer to PART–NUMBER, or whatever name we select, when the item in question is, in fact, a part number. If it should happen that a particular program accesses two different data records, each of which contains a part number field, we'll resolve this by using the COBOL qualified name technique. So, we might see a program statement such as IF PART–NUMBER of TRANSAC-TION–RECORD IS EQUAL TO PART–NUMBER OF INVENTORY-RECORD PERFORM UPDATE–INVENTORY–QUANTITY. We may not realize it, but we've just made a significant philosophical commitment. The validity of this approach is examined in more detail in Chapters 8 and 11.

We'd like each element to have a standard physical description. Part number, for example, is always a 9-character alphanumeric field. We know that some data elements, especially numbers and quantities, look different on reports and transactions than they do in files. Inventory balance is stored as a packed decimal field in the inventory record, but it appears in a display format with commas inserted and leading zeros suppressed on the stock status report. While we aren't certain, we think the dictionary is going to provide us with a solution. More research is required. For now, we'll just note the requirement.

We'd also like to record a standard definition, and if possible and necessary, the validation criteria for each element.

We need an element to element relationship. Some elements are groups that contain several more elementary items.

For instance, a lot of our dates consist of month, day, and year. Come to think of it, we also have some that are year and Julian date. Oh well, we'll probably end up with a CONVENTIONAL–DATE and a JULIAN–DATE, or something like that.[2]

We don't think we are going to need any synonyms or aliases because we are going to have all standard names, but if it ever should become necessary, we know the dictionary can handle it.

We need to relate ELEMENT to RECORD, REPORT, and SCREEN. Each ELEMENT will also be related to a USER RESPONSIBLE FOR DEFINITION. In our situation, this will be an analyst or programmer, not an end user of the data.

RECORD. Our RECORD entity represents a record in a FILE or DATABASE or SCHEMA. (If this happens to be an IMS shop, we'll have some combination of RECORDS and SEGMENTS.) Records will have names and descriptions. They will be related to the ELEMENTS they contain. They will be related to FILES (and/or DATABASEs or SCHEMAs and SUBSCHEMAs). They will be related to PROGRAMs. Each RECORD will also be related to a USER RESPONSIBLE FOR DEFINITION. (This will be an analyst or programmer, not an end user of the data.)

REPORT and SCREEN. We think REPORT and SCREEN are pretty much the same things as RECORDs. We've separated them on the diagram for clarity, but at this point we are confident that they will have the same characteristics and relationships as RECORDs.

FILE (or DATABASE or SCHEMA). Our FILE entity represents a collection of RECORDs. A file has a name and description. It has physical characteristics. We might want to record a retention period or retention requirement for some FILEs. FILEs are related to RECORDs and PROGRAMs and to USER RESPONSIBLE FOR DEFINITION.

PROGRAM. This entity represents our concept of a computer program. We think of it as a physical thing produced by the COBOL compiler. It has a name, a definition or description, a size (number of statements), and a date of last revision.

There is a PROGRAM to PROGRAM relationship, since a PROGRAM may consist of several distinct SUBPROGRAMs. We also have standard source code MODULES, so there is a PROGRAM to MODULE relationship. PROGRAMs are also related to RECORDs, FILEs, (and/or DATABASEs or SCHEMAs and SUBSCHEMAs), REPORTs, SCREENs, JOBSTEPs and of course to a USER RESPONSIBLE FOR DEFINITION. We think this same USER is responsible for program maintenance, as well.

MODULE. We've already mentioned that we have source code MODULEs. These have names, descriptions, sizes, and revision dates.

MODULES are related to PROGRAMs and to the USER RESPONSIBLE FOR DEFINITION. They may also be related to ELEMENTs, RECORDs, REPORTs, and/or SCREENs. We're not quite sure yet.

JOBSTEP. A JOBSTEP is a component of a JOB. It might be a program we've written, or it might be some kind of utility or sort program. It seems to need mainly a name, a definition or description, and USER RESPONSIBLE FOR DEFINITION.

It will relate to a JOB, a PROGRAM, and possibly one or more FILEs.

JOB. A JOB is, of course, a series of JOBSTEPs. It has a name and description. It relates to JOBSTEPs and a USER RESPONSIBLE FOR DEFINITION. It also relates to a SYSTEM, and to one or more FILEs and REPORTs.

SYSTEM. A SYSTEM is a family of JOBs, PROGRAMs, FILEs, and so on. It has a name, a description, a revision date, a USER RESPONSIBLE FOR DEFINITION. It can relate to PROGRAMs.

7.5   PROCEDURES, SOURCES OF DATA, and USES OF DATA

The next thing we need to consider is population and maintenance of the dictionary data base. Where will we obtain the data? Who will do the actual maintenance? What will be done with the data once it is captured? If we're not going to use the data for anything, why are we going to all this trouble?

The following material lists and discusses a number of topics that will have to be dealt with in one way or another. In a well-planned approach, as many issues as possible are resolved at the outset; in a poorly planned approach, they are dealt with as they arise. For the most part, they are introduced but not resolved in this chapter. There is further discussion in Chapters 8 and 11.

It is a good idea to make a distinction between the initial establishment of the dictionary and its ongoing maintenance.

7.5.1   Initial Creation

We'll discuss the initial creation of the dictionary first. The magnitude of the effort is going to depend on the number of systems, the quality of existing documentation, the degree of cooperation received from system development personnel, and so on. We'll have to take a survey and try to estimate the size of this project. Management is likely to want some estimate of the effort involved. How you develop this estimate will depend to some extent on how much you know about the organization. The more you know, the easier it should be. Here are some of the first questions we need to ask:

How many systems are there? What is the quality of system documentation? If documentation is inadequate, can the required data be obtained from the original developers or from the users? (Sometimes the people who use or maintain a system that was developed years ago don't really know very much about how it works.)

How many programs are there in each system? How good are the run books and program documentation? Have these been kept up to date as changes have been made, or do they just look good? Are job control statements kept in a single file or library? Are program source statements kept in a single file or library? Is some sort of source library maintenance system in use? If so, is library content really kept up to date? If documentation is poor, can information be obtained from the original authors? (The same thing that was said about systems is true about programs. It is even more true about programs. Often, particularly in a large shop, people are maintaining programs that they really don't understand.)

How many FILEs or DATABASEs or SCHEMAs are there in each system? How many different RECORD or SEGMENT types are there? How many different fields are there? Are standard record descriptions used, are they kept in a central library, do groups or even programmers have their own libraries? Are data element names standardized? Are the names meaningful? Are good definitions available? Is there documentation of coding structures?

How well are reports, display screens, and input transactions documented? Can the data content be obtained from user manuals? If user manuals exist, are they up to date and trustworthy?

The preceding information, once collected, will constitute the basis for an informed estimate of the size of the data collection project. Note that this doesn't directly have anything to do with the job of installing and customizing the dictionary software. While far from trivial, that job is relatively easy in comparison to the task of populating the dictionary or capturing the metadata.
There are still other questions that must be answered before we can proceed.

If the information listed above is not readily available, how will it be obtained? Who will compile it?

Who will do the actual work of preparing dictionary input? Will forms be filled out and keypunched? Will the data be entered directly on line?

Can part of the data be obtained by scanning source programs or copy libraries? If so, has software been obtained from the dictionary vendor, from another source, or written in house? This will be discussed in more detail in Chapter 11. Who will review edit lists and resolve naming discrepancies and other problems? It would be a good idea to make some test runs using the systems that are considered the best then make some runs using those that are considered the worst.

It is almost a certainty that some of the existing elements, records, files, and programs will have to be renamed. Who will do the work? How will they do it?

Now it should be possible to prioritize systems, draw up a plan for data conversion, prepare a reasonable estimate of the effort required, and get started.

7.5.2 Ongoing Maintenance

We need to think carefully about maintenance before we go too far. Once we've collected the metadata, we'll need to keep it up to date. This will involve capturing changes to old systems and programs and capturing descriptions of new systems and programs. As is the case when we look at the initial creation, there are a number of questions to ask.

How is our systems development shop organized? Do we have one group or many? Are groups organized by functional application? Are development and maintenance activities carried out by the same people? Are systems analysis activities kept separate from programming? Are job control statements and run books prepared by system developers or operations personnel?

If a data base management system is in use, are structures designed and implemented by application developers, data base administrators, or some combination of these? If there is a division of responsibility, how well do the different groups work together?

Is a formal systems development methodology in place? If so, does everyone use it? If not, are activities at all standardized? Are formal user sign-offs obtained before programming starts? Do terms like *program specification, file design*, and *program documentation* mean the same thing to everyone? If they don't, is it possible to standardize the definitions? (If everyone does things differently and standardization is not possible, we are in a lot of trouble!)

Are standards for testing and production turnover in place? If so, are they rigorously followed or are they easy to circumvent? Can the operations group refuse to accept a system or change that which is not adequately documented or tested? Do formal test data bases exist? How are they controlled?

In an ideal environment (a dictionary bigot's dream world), system developers consider the dictionary one of their most important tools. They use it as a menu of available data during the initial investigation phase of a project. They use it as a place to record data elements and definitions during the definition phase. The elements are combined into records during a physical design phase. These record definitions are then copied into programs during the program development phase. Standard routines and functions are incorporated into standard modules and subprograms, which are also kept in the dictionary and copied into programs as needed. This process automatically results in cross-references and where-used lists. This, in turn, greatly simplifies the process of change, whether it occurs during development and testing or after system implementation. Program and report generators also make use of the dictionary.

The extent to which your environment resembles this dream will have a significant effect on how you go about implementing a dictionary and will determine your success or failure.

And, there are still more questions that have to be answered.

Who will do the actual updating of the dictionary? Will it be done by the system developers or by the dictionary group? If your answer is that the developers will do it, are you sure they will accept the responsibility? Are you sure they will do the work in a timely, accurate, and standard manner?

Will input be done on line or via forms and keypunching?

Will the process of providing dictionary input be consider-ed a nuisance or a valuable activity by system developers? This will, to a large extent, be determined by the ease of using the procedure, the perceived value of the dictionary reports, the timeliness of information turnaround, and whether or not a spirit of cooperation and teamwork exists. "You must provide what I need for my dictionary in the form I specify and when I specify, and that is all there is to it!" is not necessarily the best approach. "If you provide this data in this form, here is what I can give back" might work better.

Who will set standards? How will they be policed? Can they be enforced if necessary?

7.5.3 Uses of Dictionary Data

The potential for use of the dictionary by system developers has been alluded to in the immediately preceding section. The possible benefit of evaluating the impact of change can't be overestimated. There is great operational potential, as well. A good cross-reference of files to jobs to programs is invaluable in trouble shooting, scheduling, planning to meet retention re-quirements, estimating disk space requirements, and a lot of other things.

All of this is discussed further in Chapters 8 and 11. For now, let's just repeat some things that have been said in the preceding sections of this chapter. *If you don't have specific uses for the dictionary data, why are you going to all this trouble? It is more likely that people will cooperate if they perceive that they will receive something valuable in return for their effort.* These issues need consideration at the outset. They will affect the design of the dictionary environment and the success or failure of the implementation.

7.6 A CULLINET IMPLEMENTATION

This section outlines an implementation of our simple dictionary using Cullinet's Integrated Data Dictionary. It is worth mentioning once again that the purpose is to illustrate things about dictionaries in general and that this material is not substitute for careful study of the vendor's documentation. It is also very important to note that there are usually many ways to do things. Specific choices and option selections are presented and discussed here, usually some rationale for the choice is provided. However, choices may not be at all appropriate for your particular situation. It is impossible to develop a cookbook of techniques that will work infallibly in every data processing installation and with every dictionary product. You will have to evaluate the issues and make your own decisions. The real purpose of this material is to illustrate the types of issues that arise in implementing data dictionaries.

Figure 7.2 is a diagram of the implementation using the Cullinet dictionary. Let's review each entity in turn.

7.6.1 USER

The USER entity will have USER NAME, PREPARED BY, DESCRIPTION, PASSWORD, and AUTHORITY.

USER NAME will be a 1 to 32 character name representing an individual within the data processing organization who will be responsible for some definitions within the dictionary.

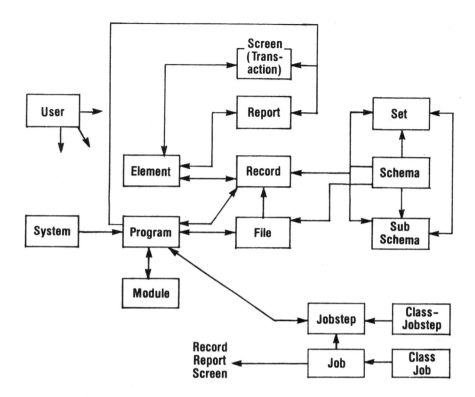

FIGURE 7.2   Cullinet Version of a Simple Dictionary

The PREPARED BY entry will indicate who created a particular USER entity occurrence. In our shop, this will always be an individual within the dictionary administration group.

DESCRIPTION is a field provided for text descriptions of dictionary entities. These can be 1 to 40 characters long. We will use it to specify the department or group in which the individual works and his or her telephone extension number.

PASSWORD will specify the password that must be used when changing anything about dictionary entity occurrences created by this user.

AUTHORITY will define some IDMS system-related capabilities for the USER.

There are other IDMS-related options that probably will have to be specified, but for the sake of simplicity we won't deal with them here.

It is worth noting several things we've done here. We've made the USER entity an individual's name. It might have been better to make it a department or group. Using a person's name is going to create an additional maintenance burden as people come and go or are reassigned. A procedure must be established to ensure that this turnover information is transmitted to the dictionary group. We expect the various managers to make use of dictionary reports as a reference showing who is responsible for what. Consequently, we expect them to be willing to send us updates, but we need to discuss this with people and obtain their agreement.

USER entity occurrences are going to be created, maintained, and deleted by the dictionary administration staff. There will also be a USER entity occurrence for each dictionary administration staff member.

We've taken the DESCRIPTION field of the USER entity and assigned a specific meaning to it. This use was not necessarily intended by the system's designers. It is probably going to be obvious to anyone who looks carefully at the reports, but we'd better document it in our dictionary procedures manual. We will probably want a special report that lists USERs and responsibilities sorted within DESCRIPTION. We might have been wiser to make use of a user-defined keyword comment or two here. For example, we could have created keyword comments named USER–DEPARTMENT and USER–PHONE for this purpose. We would also see the keywords on our dictionary reports.

The relationships between USER and the other entities will be created via USER clauses employed in creating and maintaining the other entity occurrences. It is a quirk of the Cullinet dictionary that USER can be a 1 to 32 character name but PREPARED BY is restricted to 8 characters. Because of this, all of our dictionary entities will have both. We will have two different forms of each USER name, one for each purpose.

We expect each development manager to assign responsibility for maintenance of dictionary entities to appropriate individuals. These individuals will then perform the necessary maintenance of those entity occurrences for which they are responsible. The maintenance will be audited by the dictionary administration staff. This implies that procedures are well documented and easy to follow. It also implies an ongoing training program.

PREPARED BY and USER RESPONSIBLE FOR DEFINITION will normally be the same individual, we think. We've allowed for both because PREPARED BY appears on all the standard dictionary reports and because we may find it necessary to separate actual dictionary maintenance from responsibility.

7.6.2 SYSTEM

The SYSTEM entity will represent an application system. It will provide for NAME, VERSION, PREPARED BY, USER RESPONSIBLE FOR DEFINITION, COMMENTS, and REVISION-DATE.

Name will be an assigned SYSTEM name. These entities will be controlled by dictionary administration staff, to ensure consistency and also to ensure that two different SYSTEMs never have the same name.

VERSION is included to allow for the coexistence of test and production versions.

A COMMENTS field is provided for all dictionary entities. It consists of free-form text, and there is no length limitation. We will use this for a paragraph or two of information describing the nature of the SYSTEM, its functions, and its purposes. We expect to be able to obtain these easily.

REVISION-DATE will be an installation-defined keyword comment. This means it is an addition to the standard dictionary language. It will indicate the date the system itself was revised. The dictionary will automatically record the date of actual dictionary maintenance. (This is mentioned only for SYSTEM, but obviously we might want to include it for other entities as well.)

SYSTEM to PROGRAM relationships will be established via maintenance of the appropriate PROGRAM entity occurrences.

7.6.3 ELEMENT

The ELEMENT entity will represent a data element or field. This can be the most troublesome of all dictionary entities. We will discuss a particular set of choices here; more detail on the possibilities and problems appears in the next chapter. An ELEMENT will have NAME, VERSION, PREPARED BY, USER RESPONSIBLE FOR DEFINITION, DESCRIPTION, VALUE and RANGE, PICTURE, USAGE, SUBORDINATEs, SYNONYMs, and DEFINITION.

NAME will be our standard designation for an element. NAMEs will be formed according to rules published by dictionary administration.

They will have to audit and approve new names to ensure that two truly different elements do not have the same name. Discussion of naming standards is deferred to the next chapter, but you should note now that the NAMEs will actually be used in our COBOL programs. Thus, any element name selected must conform to the rules for COBOL program names. These names will seem artificial to end users.

VERSION, PREPARED BY, and USER will be the same as for all other dictionary entities.

The DESCRIPTION field will be used for a short (1 to 40 character), English language, end-user-oriented name. DESCRIPTIONs will also be standardized and audited by the dictionary administration group. This subject is also discussed in more detail in the next chapter.

VALUE, RANGE, PICTURE, and USAGE will be used to describe the physical characteristics of and validation criteria for elements.

We are starting with the assumption that every ELEMENT will have but one unique NAME. If this is correct we will never need a SYNONYM, but we are just a little cautious about this and have decided that our procedures will provide a method for establishing and maintaining SYNONYMs just in case we need them.[3]

SUBORDINATE ELEMENTs are specified when an ELEMENT is actually a group, as in the case of a date.

ELEMENT to RECORD, REPORT, or SCREEN relationships are created via maintenance of the appropriate entity. If the physical characteristics of the ELEMENT as used in a particular place vary from the standard or base, this is handled via the appropriate RECORD, REPORT, or SCREEN definition.

It is worth noting that there are some elaborate rules regarding changes to ELEMENTs that have been included in RECORDs or REPORTs or SCREENs. It would not be desirable for the dictionary definition to differ from the actual elements stored in a FILE. Thus, careful control over changes to the physical descriptions of ELEMENTs is necessary. Some dictionary users have developed a procedure involving VERSIONs to get around this potential problem.

DEFINITION will be a text definition of the element. We expect the individuals responsible to be able and willing to provide good definitions. This is also discussed further in Chapter 8.

As is the case with other entities, we expect element definitions to be entered by the designated USERs, subject to audit and approval by the dictionary administration group. We plan to use the so-called syntax converter to scan source programs in order to get started with existing systems. We do expect it to be necessary to change many of the names, however. We have developed a detailed procedure for reviewing and scrubbing data elements on a system-by-system basis. We expect that the appropriate programmers will make the necessary program changes. Since our programmers make extensive use of interactive programming and editing tools, we don't expect this to be a lot of trouble. We believe that everyone is sold on the benefits of the dictionary and standards and will therefore cooperate.

7.6.4 PROGRAM

The PROGRAM entity will represent an individual computer program or subprogram. This entity will have NAME, PREPARED BY, USER RESPONSIBLE FOR DEFINITION, VERSION, COMMENTs, and LANGUAGE. We will also relate it to

SYSTEM, JOBSTEP, PROGRAM CALLED, MODULE USED, RECORD COPIED, and FILE.

Several things are worth noting here. First, in this dictionary, LANGUAGE is a CLASS and ATTRIBUTE structure provided with the dictionary. Second, the PROGRAM CALLED, MODULE USED, and RECORD COPIED relationships can be entered manually via the Data Dictionary Definition Language (DDDL), or they can be captured automatically via use of the precompiler. The later approach can be a significant labor-saving device and can also help us make sure that these entries are kept up to date. However, to make this work, we must establish very careful controls over NAMEs and VERSIONs. If multiple VERSIONs of the same MODULE or RECORD coexist in the same dictionary, there is a real danger that the wrong version may be copied into a program. This could cause serious problems. The IDMS precompiler, by the way, will by default copy the version with the lowest number, if no version number is specified. Thus, a reasonable rule might be to start with version 999 and decrement, so that the latest version will always have the lowest number. Another possibility is to reserve 000 for the production version. We also must make sure that programs are then processed by the precompiler—and this may create a performance problem in a large shop. If many program compiles take place during a given time period, and all must not only access but also update the dictionary, there can be significant system performance and turnaround problems. This issue is examined more carefully in Chapter 8.

7.6.5 MODULE

The MODULE entity will represent a segment of source code that may be used by many PROGRAMs. Each MODULE entity occurrence will have NAME, PREPARED BY, USER RESPONSIBLE FOR DEFINITION, DEFINITION, and COMMENTS. The actual MODULE source code can also be included if the dictionary is to be used as a copy library and if the MODULE to PROGRAM relationship is to be captured automatically.

7.6.6 FILE

The FILE entity will represent a physical file or data set. This entity will have NAME, PREPARED BY, USER RESPONSIBLE FOR DEFINITION, VERSION, and COMMENTs. We will create user-defined keyword comments for RENTENTION–REQUIREMENT and SECURITY–REQUIREMENT. FILEs can be related to PROGRAMs.

7.6.7 RECORD, REPORT, and TRANSACTION

The RECORD, REPORT, and TRANSACTION entities will represent records, reports, and screens, respectively. In this dictionary, these are essentially the same entity even though each has a different keyword identifier.

This entity will have NAME, PREPARED BY, USER RESPONSIBLE FOR DEFINITION, VERSION, COMMENTs, LANGUAGE, and ELEMENTs. If an ELEMENT that is included in one of these entity occurrences has a different physical description here than in the base definition, it will be specified here.

We can use the dictionary as a copy library for record definitions and capture the PROGRAM to RECORD relationship automatically, as discussed above. The REPORT and TRANSACTION entities are more purely informational; they will be related to PROGRAMs manually. All three entities will be related to JOBs manually.

7.6.8 SCHEMA, SUBSCHEMA, and SET

These are IDMS-related entities. They are mentioned for the sake of completeness, but since they are of interest only to a user of IDMS, they are not discussed in any detail.

7.6.9 JOB, and JOBSTEP

These two entities illustrate the CLASS and ATTRIBUTE structure provided with this dictionary. Both JOB and JOB-STEP will be defined as CLASSes or categories of information. Specific JOBs and JOBSTEPs will become ATTRIBUTEs or individual entities within these classes. We will then relate JOBSTEPs to PROGRAMs as we maintain the appropriate PROGRAM entity occurrences; RECORD, REPORT, and TRANSACTION to JOB as we maintain the appropriate RE-CORD, REPORT, and TRANSACTION entities; and JOBSTEP to JOB as we maintain the appropriate JOBSTEP occurrences.

Both of these entities will have NAME, PREPARED BY, COMMENTS, and USER RESPONSIBLE FOR DEFINITION. JOB will also have user-defined keyword comments for FREQUEN-CY, SCHEDULE, and RESTART–INSTRUCTIONS.

Once again, it is worth noting a few things that might not be obvious. PROGRAM and JOBSTEP have been kept separate because it is possible for the same PROGRAM to be used in more than one JOB. In any data base design activity, it is usually necessary to introduce an extra entity to handle many to many relationships. We should carefully examine our PROGRAM to FILE relationship and consider whether or not we should relate FILEs and JOBSTEPs instead.

The JOBSTEP to JOB relationship is an example of a relationship between two like entity occurrences, since both are actually ATTRIBUTEs as far as the dictionary is concerned.

7.6.10 Summary

It is worth repeating that the preceding material was not intended to address every detail of implementing our diction-ary design using the Cullinet product. The purpose was to show how we would approach the design problem using a specific product.

7.7 AN IBM IMPLEMENTATION

This section outlines an implementation of our simple dictionary using IBM's DB/DC Data Dictionary. Once again, the purpose is to illustrate things about dictionaries in general. This material is no substitute for careful study of the vendor's documentation. There are usually many ways to do things. Specific choices and option selections are presented and discussed here. Usually, some reasoning for the choice is provided, but these choices may not be at all appropriate for your particular situation. It is impossible to develop a cookbook of techniques that will work infallibly in every data processing installation and with every dictionary product. You will have to evaluate the issues and make your own decisions. The real purpose of this material is to illustrate the types of issues that arise in implementing data dictionaries.

The preceding paragraph probably sounds familiar. The same statement introduced our discussion of the Cullinet implementation. The following material contains even less detail than the previous section. Differences between the two dictionary implementations are emphasised more than similarities. The purpose is to illustrate how the use of a different dictionary product affects us. You will note that we will generally capture the same data. Some things will be done in a similar manner; some things will be done differently because the software is different. If we went on to look at yet another vendor's product, we would note more similarities and differences.

Figure 7.3 is a diagram of the implementation using the IBM dictionary. Let's make some general observations about the differences between it and the Cullinet implementation. Then we'll review each category in turn.

7.7.1 GENERAL COMMENTS

VERSION will not be specifically mentioned. If there is a requirement for versioning, it will be handled by a combination

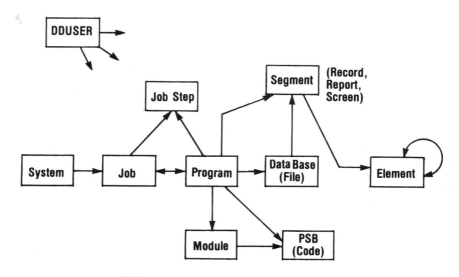

FIGURE 7.3   IBM Version of a Simple Dictionary

of the status code and occurrence number components of the name.

It is customary for users of the IBM dictionary to reserve specific lines of the DESCRIPTION and the USER DATA fields for specific purposes. For example, the first line of description is often used for the English-language name that we placed in the DESCRIPTION field of the ELEMENT entity in our Cullinet implementation.

If the IBM dictionary is going to be used as a source of record or segment definitions to be copied into programs, various special rules and procedures must be attended to. It's not worth it to describe them here.

Because the IBM dictionary is less active than the Cullinet dictionary, we do not have the option of automatically capturing relationships such as program to record. They must be maintained manually by the individuals responsible. (We could write programs that would scan program source code and generate dictionary updates if we really wanted to.) This means that we must pay very careful attention to procedures which will ensure that the dictionary is, in fact, updated when programs are revised. Otherwise our dictionary will quickly become unreliable and therefore unused. Once this sort of thing gets out of control, our dictionary project is, for all intents and purposes, finished. On the other hand, we won't have to concern ourselves with the performance issues that arise when a dictionary is highly active.

7.7.2 DDUSER

The DDUSER category will represent our USER RESPONSIBLE FOR MAINTENANCE. This category will have NAME, DESCRIPTION, and possibly USER DATA.

We have a choice regarding the full name, department, and phone number data. We can reserve specific lines of the DESCRIPTION filed for each, or we can create installation-defined attributes. We will go with the first choice because it will simplify reporting and maintenance.

If we include a security profile, it will be a part of the USER DATA. The IBM dictionary does have some specific provisions for dictionary security, but we aren't going to deal with them here.

DDUSER will be related to all other categories. If we should decide to separate the notion of USER RESPONSIBLE FOR MAINTENANCE from other forms of user, we would have several choices. We could create named installation-defined relationships for each form of DDUSER to subject relationship. We could create installation-defined attributes that would be associated with the various subjects. We could reserve specific lines of DESCRIPTION or USER DATA in each category for this information.

7.7.3 SYSTEM

The SYSTEM category will represent SYSTEMs. A NAME, a DESCRIPTION, and a REVISION DATE will be included as part of the USER DATA. SYSTEM will be related to JOB and DDUSER.

REVISION DATE could be an installation-defined attribute, but let's reserve a specific USER DATA location instead.

7.7.4   JOB

The JOB category will be used to represent our JOBs. We will have NAME and DESCRIPTION. JOBs will be related to DDUSERs, SYSTEMs, PROGRAMs, and JOBSTEPs. Our frequency, scheduling, and restart considerations will be documented in specific USER DATA locations.

7.7.5   PROGRAM

The PROGRAM category will be used to document our programs. Each PROGRAM subject will have NAME, DESCRIPTION, and LANGUAGE.

PROGRAM to SUBPROGRAM relationships will be documented via an installation-defined relationship. PROGRAMs will be related to JOBs, JOBSTEPs, MODULEs, PSBs, DATABASEs, and SEGMENTs. JOBSTEP will be an installation-defined, named relationship. As we noted in the discussion of the Cullinet implementation, the PROGRAM to JOB relationship is really many to many and requires special handling.

7.7.6   MODULE and PSB

The MODULE and PSB categories are used together to document modules. Each will have NAME and DESCRIPTION. They will relate to each other, to PROGRAMs, and to DDUSERs.

This is different from the Cullinet dictionary. The actual module source code is not included in the IBM dictionary; it will be in some separate copy library. The PSB category provides for documentation of source statements that exist in a library external to the dictionary. It is included here for that purpose. This is what might be called a quirk of the IBM dictionary.

7.7.7 DATABASE

The DATABASE category will stand for a conventional FILE as well as for any IMS DATABASE we might have. Each DATABASE subject will have NAME, appropriate physical attributes, and DESCRIPTION. We will use specific USER DATA fields to document retention and security requirements. DATABASE subjects will be related to DDUSERs and SEGMENTs.

7.7.8 SEGMENT

The SEGMENT category will be used to represent records, reports, and screens (and, of course, SEGMENTs if we have any IMS DATABASEs). We will record the difference via appropriate USER DATA notations. There are other possibilities, but that's not an important issue here.

Each SEGMENT subject will have NAME, DESCRIPTION, and various physical characteristics. SEGMENTs will be related to DDUSERs, DATABASEs, and ELEMENTs. If we elect to use the dictionary as a source of record definitions to be copied into programs, we are going to have to study the rules in the manuals very carefully.

7.7.9 ELEMENT

Last, but far from least, the ELEMENT category will be used for our data elements. Each ELEMENT will have NAME, DESCRIPTION, LANGUAGE and appropriate physical characteristics. As we've already mentioned, the actual English-language user name will be imbedded in the DESCRIPTION field. Validation criteria will be imbedded in the USER DATA. Should it become necessary to have more than one name for the same ELEMENT we will have to create ALIASes.

ELEMENTs will be related to other ELEMENTs, SEGMENTS, and DDUSERs.

7.7.10   Summary

The material presented in this section has not fully resolved every conceivable issue associated with an IBM DB/DC Data Dictionary implementation. The purpose was to illustrate how the choice of a particular product alters some of our physical design considerations. It is worth noting that extensive documentation on use of the IBM dictionary is available (See the references at the end of this chapter).

7.8   ANOTHER LOOK AHEAD

The next chapter provides a detailed review of the issues raised in this chapter. Additional concerns are also included. Chapter 10 discusses many additional things that we might choose to document in our dictionary.

NOTES

1.   A data dictionary is an excellent example of a highly flexible software package. The ability to customize software products for use at a specific installation is becoming a feature of application software as well as systems software. Many accounting, payroll, and manufacturing packages provide for user specifications of features and details. This type of product might better be thought of as a very high-level programming language. The fact that the options can be selected, and in some cases must be selected, means that decisions must be made. This means that there must be a basis for the decision. Frequently, as much systems analysis precedes a successful package implementation as would precede an in-house programming effort.

2.   If we don't clarify our notion of a data element, we will be in for a lot of trouble. Date is a good example of the sort of thing

that can really confuse us. Is date an example of a specific data element, or is it a type of element? We are going to find programs using fields like ORDER–ENTRY–DATE, SHIPPING–DATE, and so on. We'd like these to have unique names and definitions. As a matter of fact, each must have a unique name because we sometimes find several such element types in the same record type. And, no programming language allows the same name to reference different fields in a single record. The solution appears to be to think of date as a type or class of element, rather than as the same type of thing as an element like ORDER–ENTRY–DATE. At the same time, we may want to reference, or specify rules about, all dates. Techniques for doing this are discussed in Chapter 8.

3. The Cullinet dictionary software makes internal use of the SYNONYM facility. For example, when an element is copied into a record, an element SYNONYM is created. These have a tendency to pop up on dictionary reports because they cannot always be distinguished from user-created or true SYNONYMs.

References

Cullinet Software, Inc. *Integrated Data Dictionary Methodologies.* Westwood Mass.: Cullinet Software, Inc., 1982.

———. *Integrated Data Dictionary User's Guide.* Westwood Mass.: Cullinet Software, Inc., 1982.

———. *Integrated Data Dictionary: Features Guide.* Westwood Mass.: Cullinet Software, Inc., 1984.

IBM Corporation. *DB/DC Data Dictionary User's Guide.* San Jose, Calif.: IBM, 1977.

———. *DB/DC Data Dictionary Applications Guide.* San Jose, Calif.: IBM, 1977.

———. *DB/DC Data Dictionary Administration and Customization Guide.* San Jose, Calif.: IBM, 1979.

———. *DB/DC Data Dictionary Release 3: Implementation Primer.* Santa Teresa, Calif.: IBM, 1979

IBM Ltd. (U.K.). *IBM DB/DC Data Dictionary: Sample User Handbook.* Middlesex, England: IBM, 1983

8 Additional Problems and Solutions

Chapter 7 discussed a possible dictionary implementation. It had an informal narrative form; topics were considered more or less as they might arise if you set out to implement a dictionary without much prior knowledge. This chapter is organized by topic. It elaborates on some of the issues raised in Chapter 7, introduces some new material, and clarifies some of the issues that must be dealt with in a successful data dictionary implementation., Some problems are resolved here; others cannot be resolved without knowledge of the specific situation at a particular data processing shop. When we come to one of the latter, we'll discuss possibilities and questions to be asked.

8.1 THE NEED FOR ANALYSIS, DESIGN, AND PLANNING

Almost anyone would agree that implementation of any kind of computer system or program should be preceded by some

143

analysis, design, and planning. Most of us agree until someone expects us to actually do it! This is particularly true when the project in question involves a piece of purchased software. We'd like to believe that the software vendor has already done everything for us and that all we need to do is start things going.

Most data processing technicians are a lot better at planning the internal workings of some computer program than at planning how the program will interact with the rest of the organization. Often they encounter a sort of poetic justice when they realize that the software to be implemented will affect how they do business. Let's examine some premises and check them for errors.

8.1.1   The Vendor Has Already Done It All for Us

We've already had an opportunity to see some of the flaws in this reasoning. A contemporary data dictionary is an example of a new type of software package. There are some standard features, but there are also many, many options. There are ways to customize the programs and add new features. This type of software should really be thought of as special kind of programming language.

Many organizations are struggling to come to grips with the characteristics of the new systems they have purchased for accounting, manufacturing control, or whatever, because they purchased the software without realizing the implications of all its available options. Data processing personnel are often able to sit back and laugh at naive users who thought that the purchase of a piece of software would, by itself, solve some business problem. The data processing staff can laugh, until they try to come to grips with the dictionary, or the DBMS, or the application generator, or whatever software was supposed to solve all of *their* problems. Often they don't realize how much they are like the users.

It should be obvious by now that success in implementing a data dictionary requires analysis, design, and planning. The implementation will affect not only the data processing organization but the entire business. A dictionary should be thought of as a special kind of DBMS and its associated programming language. We need to do as much analysis, design, and planning as if we were going to develop a major system in house. By the time we finish spelling out all the options, we will also have done quite a bit of work that closely resembles programming.

8.1.2   We Only Need to Worry About Technical Details

How many technically superb systems have failed because they didn't meet the needs of an organization, or because the users *couldn't* adapt to them, or because the users *wouldn't* adapt to them? How many technically superb dictionaries (and DBMS packages and application generators) sit in the corner covered by cobwebs because the analysts and programmers *can't* or *won't* adapt to them?

The data dictionary is one member of a class of tools that includes data base management systems, application generator systems, design methodologies, and project management systems. Effective use of any of these tools almost always requires changes in the way a data processing shop operates—but systems analysts and programmers can be as resistant to change as anyone else.

A successful business system implementation usually has to be based on a detailed understanding of the business operation. Then it has to be sold to the people who are expected to use it. Procedures, input formats, reports, and the like must be designed so that the users see the system as beneficial, not as a nuisance. A successful implementation of a data processing support system, such as a dictionary, has to be based on a detailed understanding of the data processing operation. It has to be sold to the people who are expected to use it. Procedures, input formats, reports, and the like must be designed so that the users, who happen to be data processing staff, see the system as beneficial, not as a nuisance. Since a data dictionary implementation will change not only the data processing operation but also the entire business operation, we need to be twice as careful if we are going to succeed.

As we've noted before, computerized data processing is a relatively new discipline. The methods and procedures are still being developed. They are nowhere near as standardized as methods and procedures used by accountants, engineers, lawyers, or practitioners of just about any other discipline that has existed longer. It is far from easy to get all the people in a large data processing shop to agree on one way of doing anything. A lot of people who say they are in favor of standards really mean that they are in favor of having everyone do things their way. This is one of the biggest problems that needs to be solved if a dictionary is to be a success. Data is becoming the lifeblood of many organizations, and a good dictionary is the best available tool for managing the data. It may well be that the problem has to be solved if the organization is to succeed, but let's not sell the problem short!

8.1.3 Installing the Software Automatically Captures the Data

Getting a system up and running is only the first hurdle. Populating the data base (or files) is often a more serious difficulty. This is as true of a dictionary system as it is of any business application system. There are really two aspects to this problem: maintenance and data conversion.

Maintenance. Ongoing maintenance should be the easiest to deal with. If the analysis and design of the dictionary system has been well done, and if users support the system, procedures will be in place which will ensure that the data is kept up to date. Anyone with much experience in business systems implementation will know how much effort is required to make this reassuring statement a reality. Analysts and programmers may complain when accountants or engineers, for example aren't thrilled at the prospect of preparing transactions to update a data base, but those very same analysts and programmers often fail to appreciate the pleasures of keeping a data dictionary up to date. Fortunately, *if the design of the system and procedures has been well done*, this problem is generally minimized.

Initial Data Capture. The conversion of existing data is another story. It is always difficult and time consuming. It always involves hard work, editing and scrubbing, poring over listings of data, and preparing masses of transactions, no matter what kind of system is being created. In the case of a data dictionary system, the process can be particularly thorny. Successful conversion depends on the quality of existing documentation and the degree of standardization that already exists. If five different programs use five different names for the same data element or record or file, someone will have to recognize this and determine whether these five apparently different objects are all, in fact, the same thing. If there is no documentation containing clear definitions and descriptions, this task isn't as easy as one might expect it to be.

Software is available (and would not be that hard to write if it were not) that will scan program source code and create data dictionary update transactions. (This is discussed in more detail in Chapter 11.) However, no computer program will be capable of automatically determining that both XACCTNO7 and INP–ACCT–NO are names used for the data element VENDOR ACCOUNT NUMBER. Nor can a computer program create good definitions of data elements and files by scanning source code.

The magnitude of this problem varies greatly from place to place. Some data processing shops have excellent standards already in place; some have none. Here are some questions to ask about your environment.

Are there naming standards? If so, are the standards followed? Frequently standards are developed to satisfy auditors and managers, but they are never followed.

Do good file designs and item definitions exist?

Are there controlled libraries of program source statements? Of job control statements?

Is there a single library, or are there many?

However many libraries there are, is the content kept up to date?[1]

Can programmers or analysts or users provide good definitions? (We'll come back to this shortly.) Are they willing to? Are they genuinely just too busy to do so?

Who will review the audit listings and edit or generate the data? When will they do it?

Will this work be considered a priority project? Or will it be scheduled on an "as time becomes available" basis and thus never get done?

Once it has been recognized that two things with different names are actually the same thing, will some one alter the programs, job control statements, run books, or whatever? Who will do it? When will they do it? What priority will this work have? It could take one person several weeks or even several months to process one existing system into a data dictionary.

8.2   THE NEED FOR ANALYSIS, DESIGN, AND PLANNING - REVISITED

Data dictionary implementation projects seem to have a way of just starting to happen. Often the people who see the need are not the ones who must do a lot of the work or alter their ways of doing things. Some of these projects come out surprisingly well, but it is safe to say that the more planning, preparation, selling, and cooperation there is, the more likely the potential benefits of a dictionary will be realized. On the other hand, the less planning, the more likely it is that the dictionary administrator will be an extremely frustrated person begging for information and struggling to create and maintain a dictionary data base single-handedly. That is not a good situation to be in![2]

8.3   HOW TO GET STARTED

8.3.1 Support and Commitment Are Needed

Management Commitment. There is a glib, easy-to-make statement that is made about many kinds of activities. It goes like this: "You need management commitment to succeed with X." Activity X could be a data dictionary implementation, creation of a data administration function, use of a new data base management system, installation of a new accounting system, the start of a new training program, or almost anything. This statement is, of course, true. If one individual or group within an organization is attempting to do something that requires the support and participation of others and the others know that management does not really view the activity as important, then success is not likely.

In any dictionary implementation project, it can almost be guaranteed that the priorities and desires of the group or individual responsible for the dictionary will appear to conflict with the priorities and desires of others. Some systems analysts, programmers, computer operators, and end users will think that the time spent generating information for the dictionary is time taken away from a particular task. They may also think that the standards or procedures sponsored by the dictionary administrator are inferior to their own ideas. In some cases these perceptions may be correct; in other cases they may not be. *Building a data dictionary is a long-term activity with a long-term payoff. It may be necessary to forego some other activities which appear to have a more immediate payoff to achieve this.* It is too often true that you really can't have your cake and eat it, too. At any rate, if management does not value the dictionary project at least as much as current system development projects, decisions will be made to forego naming standards or defer compiling element definitions in order to "get the system on the air." If an organization has a truly critical need, this may even be a sound decision. But, once one exception has been made, there will probably be more. It is unlikely that anyone will ever go back and retrofit—it is not likely that a dictionary will amount to much in this sort of an environment.

Is Management Commitment Enough? Management support and commitment alone is not really enough. Management can issue edicts and policy statements, but that doesn't necessarily mean that people will act in accord with them. This may be particularly true in larger organizations. It is essential to sell the dictionary, or any other system, to the individuals who must make it work, as well as to management.

8.3.2   How to Justify a Dictionary

How can this support and commitment be obtained? In some situations, it is quite easy. In others, it is a very slow and painful process because the organization just isn't ready. Several factors can be considered in the search for justification and support.

Cost. A good manager will certainly ask for documentation of the costs and benefits of any proposed activity. Is it really worthwhile to do this? Why? We can claim that installing, populating, and maintaining a dictionary will result in cost reductions. We haven't shaken the myth that the only reason we ever install a computer system is to eliminate cost. In fact, the cost reductions used to justify a proposed implementation or purchase are often fabrications.

New computer systems usually involve increased cost in the form of computer hardware, data storage devices, computer terminals, programmers, operators, data entry personnel, and so on. These costs are usually buried in the data processing operation and are difficult to allocate to specific applications and systems. A combination of naivete and enthusiasm frequently results in a serious underestimate of these costs. This is certainly as true, perhaps even more true, when the proposed system is a data dictionary.

Cost reductions can be just as difficult to isolate and quantify. This is also true for business application systems. Suppose an inventory system incorporates a new method of predicting requirements which can reasonably be expected to reduce the number of times a customer order will be delayed in the factory due to a material shortage. Can you prove beyond a doubt that this will be true? Can you predict with any certainty how many times a year the new system will actually prevent a stock-out condition? Can you assign a specific dollars and cents value to each instance? This particular analysis could be conducted by means of an elaborate simulation. How many proposals for such a new system will be based on a proper simulation? Isn't a simulation just a very highly educated guess, anyway?

The same thing is true in the case of a data dictionary. Figure 8.1 is a list of cost-oriented justifications for a data dictionary. Let's take a detailed look at just one or two of them.

Reduced Program Development Cost

Reduced Program Maintenance Cost

Reduced Operating Costs

Use of Program and Application Generators

Ease of Troubleshooting

Reduced Documentation Cost

FIGURE 8.1   Cost-Oriented Justifications

In today's complex operating environment, application systems are highly interdependent. The purchasing system depends on data produced by the inventory system. The accounts payable system, in turn, depends on data produced by both inventory and purchasing. Suppose the inventory system terminates abnormally because of a disk hardware error. Consider the case in which file recreate and program restart instructions are readily available to the computer operator and the case in which they are not. Suppose that having a data dictionary is what makes the difference. With no dictionary, recreating the files might involve midnight telephone calls to programmers, hours of extra work on the part of data processing staff, delayed reports to warehouses and purchasing agents, a delay in sending checks to vendors, substantial losses in discounts, and so on. This is all credible. Can it really be substantiated beyond doubt that installing a dictionary will prevent such a thing? It surely won't prevent every such possibility. Nor can dollars and cents readily be assigned.

Let's examine one more item. Researching data and its availability can be a time-consuming and critical activity in any new systems project. Sometimes the necessary data already exists in some file or data base. Sometimes it may appear that the data exists somewhere, but it really is not the desired data element or there is some reason (such as the timing of updates) why it cannot be used. A data dictionary can greatly simplify this research. How much will this save?

Thus, both the new costs and the cost reductions are difficult to isolate and quantify. Some organizations will be satisfied with qualitative analysis in the form of listings similar to Figure 8.1. Some will require dollars and cents analysis. If dollars and cents are required, the best approach is to stick to data processing costs, develop reasonable cost or savings factors and multiply them by the number of programmers or reruns or whatever is at issue. Thus, a 10% reduction in systems development time multiplied by 14 systems analysts at an average salary-plus-benefits cost of $40,000 per year yields $56,000 per year. Figures like this are easy to challenge, but *if they are reasonable* they do provide a worthwhile indication of the potential benefit.

Enhanced Capability. Demonstrating enhanced capability is another form of justification. The true benefit of most computer systems is that the value of additional capabilities far exceeds additional costs. For example, it is probably true that banks couldn't process today's volume of checks, credit card transactions, and electronic transfers at all without computer systems. If this were attempted with the methods that prevailed 30 years ago, the costs would be staggering. The system probably would not function.

The existence of machine-readable files and data bases permits all sorts of analysis and simulation that would otherwise be impossible. With the advent of personal computers, spreadsheet programs, and the like, many organizations are just beginning to tap this potential.

Figure 8.2 is a listing of benefits to be realized through proper use of a data dictionary. Again, these are extremely difficult to quantify, and approaches to assigning their dollars and cents values will vary from organization to organization.

Identification of Redundancy

Provide Menu of All Data

Simulate New Systems

Strategic Data Planning

Control of Retention and Security

Centralized Data Documentation

Change Control

Identification of Synonyms

Relate Business Name to Data

Enforce Standards

Support Life Cycle Methodology

FIGURE 8.2 Justifications Based on Additional Abilities

How, Then, to Justify a Dictionary? Justification for implementation of a data dictionary is based on the same cost avoidance and enhanced capability factors as any other systems justification. Standards for this vary widely from organization to organization. Figures 8.1 and 8.2 list factors worthy of consideration. The references cited for Chapters 3 and 7 elaborate on them. There is a tendency to feel that assigning dollar values to many of these is impossible or must involve fabrication, but if the estimates are developed in a reasonable manner, they can indicate the potential value of a dictionary.

Suppose It Came with the DBMS. *Suppose you decide to purchase a system, such as IDMS, which automatically comes with a dictionary?* In this case the issue is not "Should we obtain dictionary software?" but "Should we use all the features?" Many users of products with integrated dictionaries actually make use of only the minimal capabilities. The dictionary must be used as a directory or the DBMS won't function. However, it then must be decided how far to go beyond this minimal use of the dictionary. The manner in which the dictionary is used, not used, or misused will ultimately determine costs and benefits to a far greater extent than the purchase or lease cost of the software. Even if a product of this nature has already been purchased or installed, these cost/benefit analyses should still be conducted. Proper use of the dictionary will still require commitment and justification and planning.

8.3.3   The Elements of a Plan

If you are contemplating a dictionary implementation, and your organization has a formal system development methodology or system development life cycle methodology, by all means use it. What? Use our development methodology on a project we are doing for ourselves? Does installing a dictionary really involve building systems? Yes, and yes again. Most of these methodologies provide one or more customizing steps which tailor the methodology to a particular project. This section will help with the tailoring activity. Such methodologies often contain a step (which comes after much of the analysis) in which a make or buy decision must be made. Bear in mind that writing your own dictionary from scratch is not a realistic alternative for most shops. This is discussed again in the subsection on software selection.

If you have no formal methodology, you'd best make a plan which consists, at minimum, of the steps discussed below. The basic elements of a systems design and implementation plan, as shown in Figure 8.3, are setting objectives, logical design, software selection, physical design, procedures and standards,

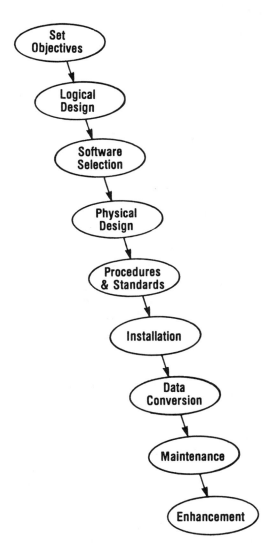

FIGURE 8.3 Elements of the Plan

installation, data conversion, maintenance, and enhancement.[3] We might also include justification and selling. In the case of a data dictionary project, this last is an ongoing activity that may have to be conducted during every step. The material that follows is a review of these key elements. We will go over them again in more detail in Chapter 11, after we've expanded on some of the issues, problems, and opportunities.

Setting Objectives. In Chapter 7 we mentioned that installing and maintaining a data dictionary is a lot of work. No one should undertake such a project without having a clear idea of the goals to be achieved. A well-understood and reasonable set of goals will also be invaluable in justifying and selling *and planning* the project.

Since a data dictionary is such an open-ended piece of software, a clear statement of objectives will also keep the scope of the project under control. It will, of course, be necessary to continually reevaluate these objectives as new opportunities present themselves. Even if no one asks for a set of objectives, it is a good idea to take the time to list them, so that *you* know what you are doing.

Sometimes this aspect is overlooked because the implementers do not realize the magnitude of the task. Sometimes the implementers take it for granted that since the dictionary is coupled with the DBMS it should be fully implemented. They do not realize that there are degrees of implementation and many alternatives.

Possibilities are as varied as organizations. If you are looking for the one absolutely correct list of objectives, you won't find it here. Chapter 7 sets forth a reasonable set of objectives for a limited implementation. These are listed in Figure 8.4. Chapter 10 suggests many more possibilities, which are among those listed in Figure 8.5. The combination of these two lists should be considered a menu that you can evaluate in terms of your needs. We will also address this subject again in Chapter 11.

Keep Track of Systems

Keep Track of Jobs

Keep Track of Programs

Keep Track of Files and Data Bases

Standardize Names

Document Data Content of Files and Data Bases

Document Data Processed by Programs, Jobs, and Systems

Document Reports and Screens

Document Modules

Document Schedules

Document Back-up and Retention

Document Maintenance Responsibilities

FIGURE 8.4   Objectives from Chapter 7

Document Sources and Uses of Data

Support Data Model

Support Information Center

Support Application Generator

Support Life Cycle Methodology

Support Distributed Processing

Document Communications Network

Maintain Hardware Inventory

Support Data Security Planning

Forms Control

Change and Problem Control

Standardize Coding and Tables

FIGURE 8.5   Additional Objectives

Logical Design. Once you've established your objectives, you should examine the entities or objects of interest that will be documented in your dictionary data base. The best way to do this is by preparing an entity relationship diagram similar to Figure 8.6. (If this looks familiar, you're right; the same diagram was included in Chapter 7.)

This step is important for several reasons. You can't possibly implement any kind of system without a good understanding of the objects to be represented in the data base. This sort of diagram is a convenient way to formalize and document your understanding. It also allows everyone involved to share the same understanding.

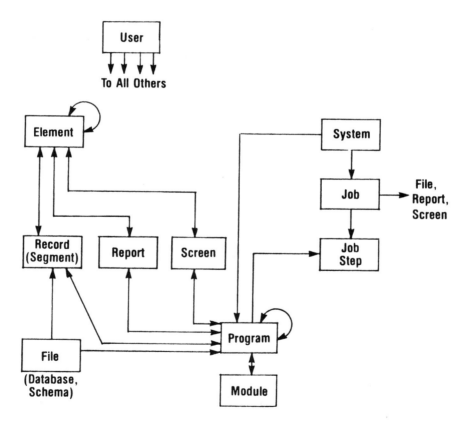

FIGURE 8.6 Conceptual Model of a Simple Dictionary

This diagram should not be based on any specific dictionary software. It should be a simple diagram showing the objects of interest and their interrelationships. We've already seen that a contemporary dictionary will offer several ways of representing anything we can conceivably decide to include. Don't get too engrossed in the workings of the software and the ideas of the builders of that software. *First, decide what it is that you would like to accomplish.*

The next step will be to document the specific pieces of data that are going to be recorded about the entities and relationships you've identified.[4] In order to do this well, you will need to take a careful look at how your organization manages data, how it manages data processing, and how it manages itself. You will need to ask how it wants do do these things and how they are currently done. You must determine whether or not the required data can be obtained. Suppose, for example, that your objective is to document data security requirements for all files and data bases. You find that no one in your organization has been made responsible for data security, and that no one has any idea which data should be secure, or why. Then, you have a problem. You might want to reconsider whether or not it is possible to achieve your objective by simply installing a dictionary.

It is safe to say that your success or failure in obtaining the type of information necessary for logical design will indicate whether you have achievable objectives and whether the organization is ready for dictionary implementation on the scale you contemplate. It is also well worth noting that if you are charged with installing and implementing a dictionary to meet certain objectives, but you can't find people elsewhere in the organization who share and are willing to work toward those objectives, then you might find a change of direction or even of employment advantageous to your mental and physical health.

Software Selection. Now you are ready to select the particular piece of software that is ideally suited to your needs. What's that? The software was already selected before you started defining objectives? Cheer up. That, by itself, doesn't have to be bad.

It is amazing how many software selection studies are really nothing but after-the-fact justifications of decisions that have been made for nontechnical reasons. Again, this doesn't have to be bad. If the software that has been selected for whatever reason is flexible and powerful enough to do the job, and the study improves our understanding of the work to be done, and the result is a successful implementation, there may be no harm.

Frequently, nontechnical criteria are as important as technical ones in software selection. A particular vendor may provide better support, perhaps because other products have already been purchased from that vendor. The new product may work well with other products previously purchased from the same vendor. If an important user or manager strongly favors a particular vendor or product for any reason at all, it may be beneficial to go along in order to have cooperation and support.

All of this is particularly true in the case of a data dictionary. If a decision has been made to purchase a particular data base management system, serious consideration *must* be given to the data dictionary provided by the same vendor. On the other hand, installation of a dictionary often involves installation of the companion DBMS. Some DBMS-independent dictionaries are available, but they are in the minority.

Suffice it to say that factors other than the capabilities of a specific dictionary product must be considered. The major dictionaries all tend to have equivalent capabilities. Beyond a certain point, debate over relative merits can only delay dictionary implementation and create unpleasantness.

Writing your own dictionary in house would be a major programming project. So much is involved in creating all the relationships, providing the flexibility that will be needed for future changes, interfacing to a DBMS, interfacing to compilers, and the like, that it just is not worth the effort in most situations.

You may think that it would be relatively simple to create a dictionary using one of the new relational data base management systems. Technically, that is possible, but it would be a lot of work. You would have to develop all the maintenance and editing logic, determine all the relationships, write a precompiler, and so on. Only a very special need could justify this approach.

Physical Design. Creating a physical design involves translating the logical design into an actual implementation of a specific dictionary. This is discussed in Chapters 7 and 10. Documentation, training, and assistance provided by the vendor are invaluable in this process.

Procedures and Standards. It is essential to develop, document, and sell appropriate procedures and standards for dictionary update and maintenance. Key issues and general principles are discussed throughout this book. Specific details must be tailored to a particular organization, product, set of objectives, and implementation. This is discussed further in Chapter 11.

Installation. Actually installing the dictionary software is an important task. Numerous parameters and options must be specified. Some reflect the physical design of the entity relationship structure; some reflect the technical details of system operation. For example, appropriate quantities of disk storage space must be allocated for data and for error recovery journals; quantities and sizes of memory for buffers and work spaces must be specified; job control language must be written. Operator documentation and instructions will be required, as well as documentation of all the options and job control language. Any special reports and screens must be prepared. Interfaces with the teleprocessing monitor must be defined. As a general rule, the vendor will provide documentation, training, and assistance that will facilitate these activities.

Many of the selections and decisions cannot be made correctly without knowledge of the quantity of data to be stored and the anticipated number and frequency of accesses to that data. As in the case with any complex system, failure to make accurate specifications will result in the need for an expensive respecification followed by a difficult data reconversion. In the case of an active dictionary, reloading the dictionary data base because not enough space was originally provided can pose a very serious problem. It may be necessary to take production systems off the air.

Data Conversion. Planning for data conversion, and actual conversion of existing systems, is discussed in section 8.1.3, in Chapter 11, and also in section 7.5.2. This conversion is a significant and time consuming activity.

Maintenance. Any large, purchased piece of software requires ongoing maintenance. Problems that occur must be evaluated and, if necessary, reported to the vendor. New releases and solutions to problems received regularly from the vendor must be evaluated, then installed. Installation of a major new release can be a major activity.

This sort of activity can keep one or two software programmers continuously busy. The number of programmers required will depend on such factors as the specific product, the size of the dictionary data base, the volume of activity, the use of features, and the number of special reports and screens required.

Enhancement. Data dictionaries are usually implemented in phases. The steps followed in the initial implementation are repeated over and over again. As use of the dictionary evolves, there will be new objectives, enhancements to the logical and physical design, new procedures and standards, and additional data conversion.

8.4 WHAT'S IN A NAME?

8.4.1 Does It Matter?

Perhaps no single issue can cause as much trouble as the need for and the establishment of naming standards. That trouble often comes as a surprise. Several factors contribute to it.

The dictionary is really a data base system. In order to maintain the data and retrieve it once it is stored, each entity occurrence must have a unique name or key. If I want to retrieve information about something I call CUSTOMER–ACCOUNT–RECORD, and three unique entity occurrences have that same name, the dictionary will show me none of them or all three of them. It has no way of knowing which I want. If I am making an inquiry at a terminal, I can examine all three sets of data and determine which is the desired occurrence, but this approach won't work if a precompiler is copying a record description into a program. As a practical matter, each data or entity occurrence must have at least one unique name.

We've seen that SYNONYMs and ALIASes make it possible for an entity occurrence to have multiple names. But, all of the names must be unique. So, if there are SYNONYMs or ALIASes, there are even more names to worry about.

We've also seen that things like version numbers and occurrence numbers and status codes can be used to differentiate between entity occurrences with the same name. But, that is really just a special way of creating a unique name. We need to know that we really want CUSTOMER–ACCOUNT–RECORD VERSION 004 copied into our program by the precompiler. This technique should be used only for situations involving data objects that are really different versions of the same basic thing. The best example of this is the case of test and production versions of a system. The test version of the record might contain an additional field. Once testing and data conversion are complete, the test version will become the new production version. Even here, it is important to have extremely good rules and procedures for controlling versions and numbers. The production version should always be "P" or 000 or 999 to minimize the possibility of error. Each software product has a rule as to which version will automatically be selected by default if none is specified.

So, in answer to the question posed in our selection heading "Yes, it does matter." We need a way to ensure that each entity occurrence documented in our dictionary has a unique name (or has unique names if we are using SYNONYMs or ALIASes).

8.4.2 Is Uniqueness Enough?

The answer to this question is *no*. Early computer programs were written in assembly languages. These were one step above absolute machine language. The names that could be used within programs were usually restricted to 6 or 8 characters. This restriction made things easier for people who designed and wrote the assembler, but it did not particularly benefit the people who wrote application programs.

The result was that, within a program, our CUSTOMER–ACCOUNT–RECORD might be referred to as CUSTACCT or CUSTREC or C1234 or anything else that occurred to an individual programmer. Whether C1234 would mean anything to the next person who looked at a particular program was not considered a very important question. In fact, it was highly likely that one programmer would write a program that used the name C1234 while another would use CUSTACCT. This would be a problem for anyone looking at both programs. Suffice it to say that a desire for consistency in naming is one of the big motivations for developing naming standards, copy libraries, and data dictionaries.

Frequently we encounter what we might think of as families of names. For example, CUSTOMER–ACCOUNT–RECORD might consist of CUSTOMER–ID–NUMBER, CUSTO-MER–NAME, CUSTOMER–STREET–ADDRESS, CUSTOMER–CITY, CUSTOMER–STATE, CUSTOMER–ZIP–CODE, and CUS-

TOMER–ACCOUNT–BALANCE. In practice, there would be probably be more elements—but we can get in enough trouble with these.

This is worth spending some time on. Let's refer to Figure 8.7. First of all, we have defined something called a customer account record. It has particular characteristics and consists of particular data elements or fields—identifying number, name, street address, city, state, zip code, and account balance. Each of these elements or fields has particular characteristics. The record is to be contained in a particular file or collection of related records. The file will be stored on a particular disk or tape and will be processed by one or more programs. There can be different versions or generations of the file. If we add and delete customers once a month, for example, there will be a January version, a February version, and so on. Notice that in this context, the word version has a slightly different meaning from its meaning when used as a dictionary keyword.

For a general conversation between two people, the preceding might be adequate. For computer programming, it is not. There must be a linkage which ensures that when we write a COBOL statement such as MOVE CUSTOMER–NAME OF CUSTOMER–ACCOUNT–RECORD to CUSTOMER–NAME OF CUSTOMER–STATUS–REPORT we are referencing the 11th through 45th positions of the customer record and the 21st through 55th positions of the report. We must ensure that the program is accessing the customer account record contained in the customer status file and not some other file. If it is the month of March, we must ensure that we have the copy of the file that was created on March 1. The names that we use must follow the rules of the COBOL programming language, but as long as we are consistent within our program, the COBOL system will work fine. It will not prevent us from using names which are different from those used in any other program.

A requirement that our program must use the description of the record that is contained in a particular copy library or data dictionary will tend to force us to use the same names that everyone else uses. *This, of course, requires that there be a unique name which we can use to call for the definition, and that we have some way of finding out what that name is.* We

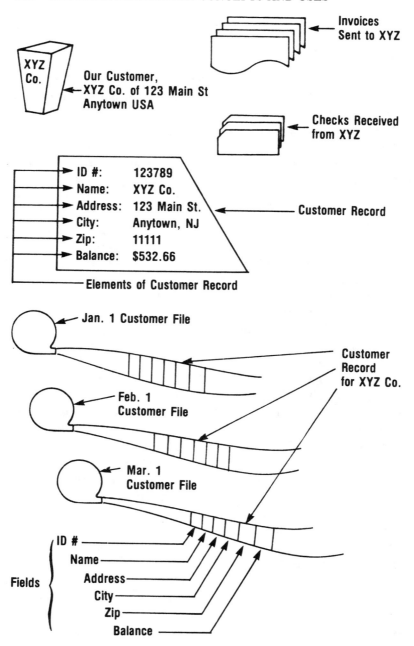

FIGURE 8.7   Entities and Records

might have to understand the significance of CUST–STAT–CUST–REC VERSION 002, NEW–CUST–CUST–REC, and on and on.

It can be extremely helpful if the name itself helps us understand what object it stands for. We've mentioned before that confusion regarding which name really stands for which data item is a big source of programming errors. However, no matter how descriptive and unambiguous the names are, an English-language text definition will also be needed. Of course, we will provide for this in the dictionary—that is, we will provide a place for it. Someone must write and feed it to the dictionary.

There is more. Take another look at the example we've been reviewing. It exemplifies concepts of naming. We talk about street addresses, cities, zip codes, and so on. We are comfortable talking about these things and their characteristics: "A zip code is a 9 digit number that . . . ." It also exemplifies the notion that there are particular names, addresses, and so on that belong to or describe or go with something called a customer. *Normally it doesn't bother us much that a customer zip code and a vendor zip code are two different instances of the same sort of thing.*

Looking a little more closely, we note that there is a specific instance of the customer zip code that is contained in a particular location in something called a customer record. Furthermore, there may be other types of customer records. There is also a specific instance of a vendor zip code that is contained in a particular location in something called a vendor record. There may also be more than one type of vendor record. These separate data fields share certain characteristics because each is intended to contain a representation of a zip code. They also are truly separate fields in separate records.

Thus, we need a unique and meaningful name for the zip code field that is contained in the customer record that is contained in the customer status file. This name must, by the way, conform to the rules of a specific programming language. In a COBOL program we might want to use CUST–STAT–CUST–ZIP-CODE. In a Pl/I program we might use the nearly identical CUST_STAT_CUST_ZIP. In an assembler or Fortran program we might be forced to use CSTZIP. One last thing. It isn't a good idea to try to discuss CSTZIP, or even CUST–STAT–CUST–ZIP, with a sales manager or accountant.

8.4.3 What's in a Good Name?

The first thing that needs to be established is that most, if not all, of our dictionary entities will require at least two names. One name will be for use in computer programs, job control language, and so on. The other will be for use in conversations between human beings, especially between human beings who are not computer programmers.

As a general rule, contemporary data dictionaries do not directly provide for the latter name. This is a source of considerable confusion and unnecessary debate. The problem is usually resolved by using some specific comment or description area for the English-language name and placing a computer-oriented name in the dictionary's actual name field. This is what we did in the example in Chapter 7. The latter names, by the way, are restricted to 30 characters or so in most dictionaries, because few programming languages provide for longer names.

Most dictionaries do provide for language-specific SYNO-NYMs or ALIASes. This is usually less of a problem.

The next thing we'd like to be able to do with our dictionary is locate all occurrences of zip code, or date, or shipping date, or what have you. This is where the real fun starts. Try to come with a 30 character name that clearly exemplifies the Julian format, promised (not actual) shipping date for a customer order as represented in the customer order record, which is contained in the open orders file of the shop schedule system. Ask two different people to do this; then tell them that they must agree on a single name. If you aren't convinced that naming causes problems, be sure you do try this experiment.

8.4.4 Possible Solutions

One and Only One Name. Some integrated data base purists will insist that there is in fact one data element called zip code, that this element must appear exactly once in the dictionary with an appropriate name such as ZIP–CODE, that it can have only one physical description, and that any record or program which processes zip code is, in fact, processing a copy of that element and must use the approved name. This is a great idea, but there are a lot of practical problems with it.

First of all, this approach will work really well only if we do, in fact, have but one type of zip code data element in our data base. That will never be true. We will have to deal with customer zip code, vendor zip code, employee zip code, and so on. Even then, this approach will work well only if there is really but one record type in our data base that contains the customer zip code. For most organizations, this is an impossible dream.

One and Only One Name Most of the Time. Another approach is a variant of the one we just described. The standard name is used as frequently as possible. When ever possible, the COBOL qualification is used to differentiate between two fields that would otherwise have the same name. When this is not practical, a prefix or suffix is used to distinguish between ZIP-CODE and CUST–REC–ZIP–CODE or whatever.[5] Generally in this situation, the prefix or suffix is expected to be chosen from an ''approved'' list. However, the 30 characters or so often just won't be enough for some element, and it will be necessary to create an abbreviation. Naturally, the abbreviation must also be selected from an ''approved'' list.

This approach can create a lot of problems and inconsistencies unless things are well managed. We'll see that what is probably the best solution is really a variation of this—so we'd better plan on managing names carefully.

Qualification: A different variant provides a prefix which identifies the applications area, and in the case of a data element, a prefix which identifies a record. Thus, the customer record used primarily for accounts receivable might be called

AR–CUSTOMER–REC, while the customer identifier contained therein might be called AR–CUST–CUST–ID. This last, somewhat awkward name indicates that we are dealing with a customer identifier contained in a customer record used primarily by an accounts receivable system. CUST–ID, CUST, and AR would all be selected from a list of standard abbreviations.

This approach has the advantage that one can look at a name and immediately have some understanding of the thing it represents. However, it is extremely distasteful to the integrated data base purists because it implies that there is not a single integrated data base containing but one customer identifier field and may never be one. Is this premise valid or invalid in your situation?

A practical disadvantage is that maintaining the list of standard abbreviations and enforcing the standards can be very cumbersome and difficult, particularly in a large shop.

What Is a Good Solution? The key step toward a good workable solution of these naming problems is acceptance of the following facts:

> The name that has been getting all this attention is an artificial name that is contrived for use by computer technicians. It is necessary to contrive this sort of name because of the nature of contemporary programming languages and data processing practice.
>
> It is, in fact, the name of an entity that exists within some computerized system. That is, we have been talking about the name of a particular field, or record, or file, or program, or system.
>
> Many of these entities are, in turn, representations of other things that exist in what might be called the real world.[6] Some of them have meaning only within the context of the computer system.
>
> The real-world entities have names like "customer identifier used by the accounts receivable section." Sometimes

we can shorten this to "customer identifier" if the context is clear. Psychologists and logicians who study the ways in which we know and understand things theorize that this is, in fact, the way we think. Figure 8.8 illustrates this concept by drawing boxes within boxes. Figure 8.9 shows the same concept in the form of something called a "semantic network."[7] This theory has direct application to our problem, but don't forget that real-world entities clearly do not have names like "AR–CUST–CUST–ID."

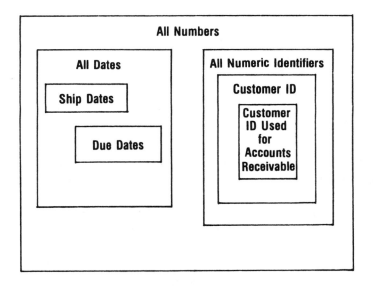

FIGURE 8.8 Categories within Categories

We would like to use the dictionary to capture the information that there is a real-world class of entity called customer, that the AR–CUST–RECORD is one of several data processing entities which contain information about customers, that we have assigned identifying numbers to customers as a data processing convenience and that the AR–CUST–CUST–ID field of the record in question is put there to contain a particular type of information.

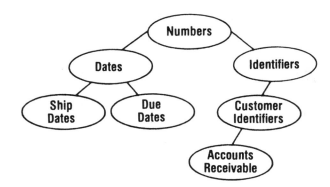

FIGURE 8.9   Semantic Network

We often need to be able to locate all occurrences of detail elements which represent similar things. The zip code we've been belaboring is a good example of this.

Several things follow from these observations. First, the name field provided by the dictionary can't carry the freight all by itself. This does not mean that we shouldn't try to standardize names. Names still do have to be unique, so we should adopt as reasonable a standard as we can. The AR–CUST–CUST–ID technique isn't bad. The "of language" is a reasonable alternative.[8] The exact standard that you select in your shop is going to depend on your unique situation. Ask these questions:

Were any standards in existence before the inception of the dictionary project? If so, are they usable? If so, use them. Why invent and implement new standards?

How big and diverse is the data processing operation?

Are there many distinct applications? The prefixing or suffixing technique provides a good way to handle this.

Are there shared files or data bases? In this case, application prefixes do not make sense. Subject-oriented prefixes or suffixes may still make sense.

Are management and data processing staff receptive to and supportive of standards? Can you successfully implement a dictionary if they are not? Perhaps you'd do well to stop working on standards and go back to selling.

Will it be necessary to make a lot of program changes?

Is it realistic to talk about making these changes?

By the way, it is interesting to note that data element and field names usually cause the most trouble. It can be surprising, really surprising, how much heat this issue can generate. Record names are troublesome, but much less so. File, program, and system names don't seem to be nearly as troublesome.

The second major consequence of the facts we cited at the beginning of this section is that we need some other way for getting at the name of the real-world entity represented by one or more data processing entities and of maintaining the cross-reference. We've already noted that many dictionary users employ a description or comments field for this purpose.

It is still a good idea to have standard words to be used in this name. Why? Because we still would like to know that we are talking about an identifying number, that this particular identifier leads us to a customer, and that it is the customer identifier that is used for accounts receivable purposes.

Let's examine one other pair of alternatives before we leave this topic. We could make sure that the real-world name contains appropriate classifying words and then make use of the dictionary reporting facilities to search, scan, or sort when we want to find all customer identifiers. Then the name of a date field would always contain the word "date," the name of an identifier field would always contain the word "identifier," and so on. We could find all customer identifiers by searching for the keywords "customer" and "identifier."

Alternatively, we could use dictionary extensibility (the Cullinet CLASS and ATTRIBUTE structures, for example) to create actual linkages among data processing entities which stand for the same type of real world object. This alternative will surely make dictionary maintenance more difficult. It will also cause dictionary processing to use more of our computer resources. The former alternative, while more susceptible to error, seems adequate and less expensive.

In either case, don't forget that with contemporary technology, the keywords must be assigned or the relationships must be established by some human person with an understanding of the data. This is not a trivial requirement.

What Is a Good Definition, By the Way? Each dictionary entity has a definition as well as a name. How easy will it be to obtain good definitions? To answer that question, we must ask another: What are the characteristics of a good definition? Answer: It must be clear, complete, correct, and meaningful. Which of the following do you like better?

CUSTOMER–CODE identifies the customer.

CUSTOMER–CODE is a customer identifier. A unique number is assigned to each customer by the marketing department. The first three digits of the number identify the sales region that initially entered the customer data. A customer may subsequently be serviced by other sales regions, but the identifier is not changed. The next five digits are selected from a list of available numbers maintained for the sales region. The final digit is a mod 11 check digit which is calculated by . . . .

A good definition will also discuss origination, validation criteria, and any special rules or characteristics. It is surprisingly difficult to get people to write good definitions. Definitions must be audited.

Don't Forget the Purchased Packages. The names used within purchased packages probably will not conform to your standards. Since it is not a good idea to make extensive modifications to purchased packages, it is not a good idea to change them.

If you choose to document the names within purchased packages, you'll have to live with nonstandard names in your dictionary. You'll also have to use versions or prefixes or suffixes to keep these names distinct from names of your own or names used in other packages.

What, Then, is the Answer? There may be no single best answer. We offer a workable solution in Chapter 11. You'll have to decide whether it suits your situation.

Is It Stored or Calculated? Here is another important thing about data elements. Many of the elements that appear on reports and output screens are never stored in any file or data base. They are derived or calculated from other data elements. Should these be included in the dictionary? Of course. How should they be named? A good standard will provide for these as well. Shouldn't the definition include the formula or method of derivation? Certainly it should; otherwise it isn't a good definition. Finally, we'd better have some keyword or class-word or attribute that identifies a calculated element as such.

8.5 AGAIN, WHAT ABOUT VERSIONS?

While this is a much less esoteric topic than the philosophy of naming, it is one which also requires careful attention.

Often a systems development group is working on modifications to a production system. The modifications may involve changes not only to programs but to files, records, and data elements as well. If the dictionary is active, or if the dictionary is used as a copy library, or if dictionary maintenance proceeds in concert with the rest of the development activity, it will be necessary to maintain multiple definitions of the same data processing entities and keep them straight.

Even if this were not the case, versions would be necessary. Most dictionaries implement elaborate rules that prohibit changes to production entities or prohibit changes to the physical descriptions of fields that are contained in records.

These restrictions are very reasonable, particularly in the case of an active dictionary.

In any event, it is necessary to develop a change procedure that takes this into account. Normally this will consist of creating new versions of the dictionary entities involved, and then, when testing and validation are complete, deleting the production versions and replacing them with the new ones.

If a need for further change is discovered during testing, more than one test version may sometimes exist. Controlling and coordinating versions of various entities, including modules, by the way, can be a significant task during a large development project. It also becomes important to make sure that the actual file or data base and the description used by a particular program do actually match. This is a problem whether or not there is a dictionary. The dictionary and the associated procedures should help keep this under control.

This is not an unusual problem, nor is it trivial. Data base and file design changes are all too common in large development projects. We'd like to think that good, up front, design activities will always eliminate the need for design changes, but for whatever reason, the need for such changes must be dealt with. Suppose there are 20 programmers working on 50 or 100 programs and it becomes necessary to add 2 new data elements to each of 3 different record types. Here is what must be done.

The element descriptions, definitions, validation rules, and coding structures must be added. If a dictionary is being used, they must be added to the dictionary. If the only documentation is hand-written, they must still be added to the hand-written documentation. It is probably easier and more effective to use a dictionary.

The relevant record definitions must be altered. This also is true whether or not a dictionary is in use. If there is a central copy library, it must be revised. If, heaven forbid, each individual programmer has been allowed to or required to write unique record definitions, all of them must be located and altered.

It is necessary to determine which programs and modules are affected, to change them, and to recompile them. A well-maintained dictionary can really simplify this job.

The files or data bases that have been created for program and system testing must be recreated in the new format. It is very possible that a project team of this size would be using more than one test data base. It is also unlikely that all programs could be altered simultaneously without seriously affecting schedules. Consequently, it may really become necessary to have two different test versions of things operable at the same time.

In this type of situation the combination of a well-thought-out dictionary implementation and a good set of procedures for change control can save a lot of trouble.

8.6 ACTIVE/PASSIVE and AUTOMATIC/MANUAL

We've already noted that some dictionaries are highly active, some dictionaries are semi-active, and some dictionaries are highly passive. This would certainly be a factor in product selection if we were free to select any product. Even when we do not have this freedom, there are still decisions to be made. How many of the active features of the dictionary should be used?

Operating efficiency and hardware resource availability are important considerations. A data dictionary is a complex data base. There are many interrelationships among the data records contained in the dictionary data base. Updating, and even retrieving data from this data base frequently involves a lot of processor activity and a lot of disc activity. In a large shop with many programmers, or in a small shop with limited hardware resources, it just may not be possible to fully utilize the active features of your dictionary.

This is particularly true of the ability to capture program to data cross-reference information during program compilation. You may find that your vendor or salesperson will be strangely silent about this, or you may be advised that there is no problem. In your particular situation, that may be true. The best thing to do is run some carefully controlled and closely observed tests on your system—*before* you do a lot of planning. You should use system measurement tools and subjective observations of compile times to make this evaluation.

The preceding should not be interpreted as a statement that active dictionaries are unworkable. A completely passive dictionary implementation results in serious update problems. Analysts and programmers with deadlines to meet are not particularly interested in devoting much effort to the maintenance of a passive dictionary. As a result, dictionary maintenance is likely to be done very late, if at all. It is also likely to be inaccurate. Left to their own devices, analysts and programmers often are not very careful about naming standards. Consequently, given a passive dictionary, the entity names used in the programs may not match the names in the dictionary to the extent that it is impossible to correlate the data.

An active dictionary that serves as the single, central repository of metadata and that automatically captures cross-reference data can, if used properly, solve many of the problems inherent in a passive implementation.

So, what is the answer to these problems? Sad to say, there may be no single right answer. Ask the following questions.

What will the impact be on the performance of your system? This question should be asked for each optional feature.

What is your commitment to use of the dictionary? Have the right people been sold on the benefits of the dictionary to the extent that additional hardware can be purchased to support it?

Is it possible for a passive system to function in your environment? Is there sufficient user commitment to ensure that a passive dictionary will be updated correctly and in a timely manner?

If data is not captured automatically, who will perform the maintenance?

Use of the dictionary as a copy library results in what might be called an automatic audit of its content. Who will perform the audit of a passive dictionary?

The use of system development tools is an important factor here. More and more vendors are offering query, report-generating, program-generating, and even application-generating tools that rely on an associated dictionary. Use of one of these tools implies an active dictionary system. There is no choice. (This is as good a place as any to reiterate that selection of dictionary software, selection of data management software, and selection of productivity tools are not separate and distinct issues. They are becoming more and more interrelated.)

Our final words on this subject are that implementation of a dictionary requires looking at the entire data processing environment, that the active versus passive issue is important, and that it is necessary to make sure that the solution adopted will be workable in a particular environment.

8.7 TECHNICAL and OPERATIONAL ISSUES

In all cases, the vendor's technical documentation will cover purely operational considerations in detail. These include system generation, calculation of memory and disc space requirements, job control language, dictionary maintenance language and rules, necessary sequence for adding entity occurrences to the dictionary, interface to teleprocessing monitors, back-up and recovery of the dictionary data base, journalling requirements, reorganization of the dictionary data base, report generation, console operator procedures, and relationship to other software components.

The information provided by the vendor should be studied carefully. Then appropriate procedures and documentation should be developed.

Here are a few things that could be overlooked.

Will the dictionary always be running? If it is highly active, the answer to this is probably yes. Then starting the dictionary must be a part of system initialization.

Will reports be produced automatically on some predetermined schedule? Will they be triggered by specific events, such as the implementation of a new system? Will they be on a run on request basis? Who will initiate the jobs to produce the reports? How will they be distributed? How will special requests be handled?

How will dictionary problems be reported and resolved?

Will computer operations think of the dictionary as a production system, or will they think of it as something the programmers run?

Will procedures for the turnover of new systems or system changes incorporate steps that will ensure that the dictionary has been correctly updated? This can be critical.

Obviously, these also are issues that need to be resolved in light of procedures already in existence, degree of commitment to the dictionary, and so on.

8.8 SECURITY CONCERNS

Today's dictionaries provide facilities for implementing passwords and security. This is an important issue. The dictionary will contain valuable data about the operation of the data processing shop and also about the operation of the entire organization. It is highly desirable to prevent unauthorized access to this metadata. It is also important to prevent unauthorized modification. Given a highly active dictionary, a disgruntled employee could wreak havoc on the data processing operation.

These security procedures generally rely on user codes and passwords that restrict access to the entire dictionary, to specific entity occurrences within the dictionary, or to the use of specific dictionary features.

The security provided as a part of the dictionary will be adequate only if it is used intelligently. Here are some relevant questions and comments.

Who should be allowed to access what? Can project teams alter data that they think of as their own?

Will passwords be controlled and changed from time to time? Will they be changed when employees leave or are discharged?

Will the users of the system exercise proper discretion regarding security of the passwords themselves?

Does the overall computer system provide some sort of data security that will prevent access to dictionary data via means other than the dictionary software?

Don't forget that the systems programmer or dictionary administrator will probably need access to everything.

Don't forget that too much security or poorly designed security procedures can make everyone's job more difficult while providing few, if any, real benefits.

8.9 HOW MANY DICTIONARIES?

Multiple dictionaries are starting to become a fact of life at many installations. Vendors are beginning to provide for this in the software. There are several reasons for this phenomenon.

If data management or application-generating software relies on the data contained in the dictionary data base, and this software is run on more than one processor or multiprocessor complex, there is a need for a dictionary at each. Shared disc systems and distributed processing configurations can be considered as alternatives, but frequently there will be so many operational problems that this is not a real alternative.

If there are processors at geographically separate locations, multiple dictionaries will almost certainly be a necessity.

Operating efficiencies can be gained by separating dictionaries, because fewer users will be contending for a single resource.

There are security benefits. Data in a separate dictionary can be more easily controlled.

It is particularly beneficial to separate a production dictionary from one or more test dictionaries.

Naturally, if there are going to be multiple dictionaries, it will be necessary to think about what will be in which dictionary, how the content of the various dictionaries will be controlled and coordinated, and how data will migrate from one dictionary to another.

In most situations, there will be a need for one master dictionary that will contain, among other things, documentation of the location and content of all other dictionaries.

There will be a need for one dictionary associated with each processor or multiprocessor complex. This will contain the metadata needed by the people and processes that make use of that system. In a distributed processing environment, it will also contain metadata that describes and locates other processors and processes with which the processor must communicate.

There will often be justification for one or more test dictionaries.

Once again, there is a need for careful planning and for well-thought-out, well-documented procedures. And, once again, the exact nature of the solution depends on the specific organization.

Some general principles can be offered.

There must be a global or master dictionary.

No dictionary, with the possible exception of the master dictionary, should contain more metadata than is needed for the operation of processes local to its processor. Analysis of these needs requires knowledge of what runs where.

Procedures and controls must be installed to ensure that all dictionaries are updated when necessary and that the content of all dictionaries is consistent.

The migration of metadata from one dictionary to another must be provided for. The migration of data from a test environment to a production environment is particularly critical. Procedures for this must be integrated with procedures for program turnover.

8.10 ORGANIZATION

Who will be responsible for doing what? A clear division of duties and responsibilities among various groups is essential. We offer guidelines in Chapter 11.

8.11 SUMMARY

This chapter has elaborated on a number of the practical considerations raised in preceding chapters. It has also raised some new issues. It should serve to demonstrate that implementation of a data dictionary is a major systems development project. It also demonstrates that such a project cannot be addressed in a vacuum. The overall data processing and business operation must be taken into consideration.

The next chapter discusses possibilities for extending the dictionary design discussed in Chapter 7.

NOTES

1. Many data processing installations have established central copy libraries. This is done to maintain control over the source code for production programs. It is also done so that copies of source programs may be secured in a safe place by copying the central library at regular intervals. However, programmers have a tendency to neglect maintenance of the central copy library. Sometimes it is because they must work under extreme pressure; sometimes it is just plain carelessness. At any rate, it is safe to say that it there are not adequate procedures to ensure that the library is kept up-to-date, or if the procedures are not rigorously enforced, the central library will not contain correct, up-to-date source programs or job control statements.

2. This is not at all unusual. Often the individual responsible for dictionary maintenance is left out of the system development process, considered a nuisance by most of the systems development staff, and generally ignored and frustrated. This can be the result of lack of organizational commitment, a poor selling job, or a poorly designed dictionary environment.

3. These are really the basic elements of planning for any system. Any life cycle or development methodology will contain these elements, called by one name or another. Each of these tasks must and will be performed. Often this is not recognized and they are performed informally. This approach is rarely as efficient as a more organized one.

4. People versed in the jargon of data administration and data dictionaries frequently state that data fields or data elements are the representations of attributes of entities. This is not always true. Sometimes they represent membership in categories. Sometimes they represent relationships to abstract concepts. This is particularly true of the so-called attributes of our dictionary entities.

5. Many good programmers have been using the prefixing trick for years. It can really help keep things straight within a program. For examples, see Tyler Welburn, *Structured COBOL: Fundamentals and Style* (Palo Alto, Calif.: Mayfield Publishing Co., 1981). Many other programming texts could be cited.

6. For detailed discussions of this type of problem, see William Kent, *Data and Reality* (Amsterdam, The Netherlands: North-Holland Publishing Co., 1978) and S. I. Hayakawa, *Language in Thought and Action* (New York: Harcourt Brace Jovanovich, 1978). Both are concerned with semantics and the true significance of names.

7. See, for example, Colin Martindale, *Cognition and Consciousness* (Homewood, Ill.: Dorsey Press, 1981).

8. This is discussed in Chapter 15 of the *DB/DC DATA DICTIONARY Implementation Primer* cited in the references for Chapter 7.

9 A Look Back

In Chapters 1 and 2, we reviewed some data-related problems and some potential solutions. Now that we've looked over a number of data dictionary concepts, let's go back and see how the concepts relate to the problems and possible solutions. We've already noted that you shouldn't be trying to implement a data dictionary because it's fashionable, or because it came with a data base management system, or because some authority said everybody should have one. You should have a clear idea of what it is you hope to accomplish and why.[1] This chapter will help you evaluate some potential benefits. As much as possible, the sequence of topics matches the first two chapters.

This chapter also contains a lot of questions. Answers are discussed in Chapters 10 and 11. Finding your own answers to these questions is a key element in the development of your plan for using a data dictionary.

9.1   REDUNDANT DATA

It is often considered a data truism that redundancy is bad. Actually, that isn't always the case. Sometimes there are performance, integrity, or security considerations that make redundancy necessary. Only *unplanned, uncontrolled,* or *undiscovered* redundancies are really bad.

To eliminate or control redundancy, you must first be aware of it. That means you need to know whether two data fields or groups of data fields are or are not representations of identical information.

Next, if redundancy exists, you need to determine whether it should be eliminated or controlled. To do this you have to find out who uses the information, how they use it, when they use it, and where they use it. You need to know if there is a good reason for redundancy. Often, redundancies are introduced to resolve performance problems. A designer might decide to store a frequently used data element that could be calculated because many time-consuming disc accesses would be involved in the calculation.

Finally, you must decide how to eliminate or control the redundancy. It is not unusual to create an extra copy of a file or data base in order to avoid processing conflicts. This is particularly common when it is necessary to run reports or queries concurrently with on-line updates.

You will need to know where all copies of the data are stored; how they are stored; which programs, jobs, and systems access which copies; when and how each copy is updated; and the implications of any proposed changes.

Elimination of redundancy will involve modifying or re-writing programs and systems that access or maintain the data. It will probably involve changes in computer operating procedures, which in turn will require changes to run books and other documentation. Elimination of redundancy must also involve changes in end user operating procedures. Often different copies of the same data will have been maintained by different user groups. If copies are eliminated, procedures and user guides will of necessity change. You may find that no one wants the responsibility, or you may find that no one wants to relinquish control.

Control of redundancy involves introducing routines or programs or procedures which ensure that all copies are updated when any one copy is updated. It is also necessary to introduce routines or programs or procedures that compare versions and identify discrepancies. When discrepancies are encountered, it is necessary to determine which is correct and make the required adjustments. Often this is not as easy as it sounds. It can be very difficult to determine which is correct. Negotiating the responsibility for correction can involve acrimonious debate.

In many data processing shops, obtaining the information required for these steps is a tall order. Figure 9.1 is a copy of Figure 7.1. (Chapter 7, you will remember, presented our conceptual model for a simple dictionary.) You should take a minute or two to look over this figure and refresh your memory. What will you accomplish by implementing a data dictionary like this? You will know which fields in which files or data bases are accessed by which programs. You will also know how the programs relate to jobs and systems. Ask yourself the following questions:

Will your element names and definitions and your use of synonyms or aliases enable you to identify all occurrences of the same information?

Will you be able to identify situations in which elements that appear to represent the same data really represent different versions of the data—such as quantity shipped this month and quantity shipped this year?

Will you be able to identify all occurrences of the same type of information—all dates, for example?

Will you know which elements are calculated or derived, and how they are calculated or derived?

Will you know the original sources of all elements?

Will you know all uses of all elements?

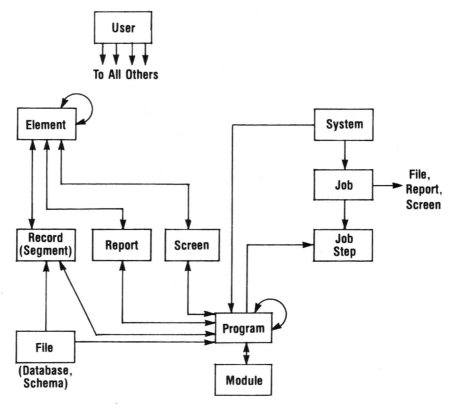

FIGURE 9.1   Conceptual Model of a Simple Dictionary

Will program to program data transfers be identified?

Will good naming standards help? In this context, what is a good naming standard?

How could keywords or some sort of indexing help?

How could the extensibility features of your data dictionary help?

Will you know who really uses the data and how?

Will you know the processing schedules for the jobs that contain the programs?

If you cannot answer "yes" to each of these questions, you cannot implement this model dictionary. You should determine what must be done to obtain the missing information and make that a part of your plan. The less desirable alternative would be to side step the issue by limiting the scope of your dictionary.

9.2 INCONSISTENT DATA AND REPRESENTATIONS

Consistency really derives from control of redundancy. Thus, everything discussed in the preceding section is relevant in this section as well. In the effort to eliminate inconsistent data, ask these additional questions:

> Can the dictionary implementation we've developed so far help you determine whether there are procedures or programs to ensure consistency?
>
> Does it provide for validation rules and criteria?
>
> Does it provide for data consistency and integrity rules?
>
> What about procedures to ensure that such rules are actually entered in the dictionary?

Can the data dictionary help eliminate inconsistent representations? We should be able to use it to document things in such a way that these will not occur—or at least not as often and not without our being aware of them. How can we accomplish this? We can add documentation of coding structures and cross-references from codes to data elements containing coded information to the uses of the coded data.

9.3 COMPLEXITY AND INTERDEPENDENCE

We can deal with complexity in two ways: we can reduce it or we can make complex things easier to understand. Complexity can be reduced by eliminating redundancy. It can also be reduced by eliminating reports or screens that contain the same information, no longer have any useful purpose, or are not even used. We need to ask the following questions:

Does the dictionary we've developed so far help us determine who actually uses the reports or screens?

Does it help identify screens and reports that really contain the same information?

Does it help us identify the tasks and procedures that require use of the information contained in the reports and screens?

If we can't eliminate a complexity, we might at least hope to understand it better. Does this first version of the data dictionary identify dependencies between programs and jobs? It does tell us which ones use the same data bases or files or data elements.

9.4   DIFFICULTY OF CHANGE

Anything that reduces or simplifies complexity should make change easier to deal with. Anything that reduces or identifies redundant data should do the same. The dictionary we've developed so far will help us determine which programs are affected if we change a file or data base. Will it help us determine which data elements are affected if a particular business procedure or requirement changes? Will it help us determine which reports or screens or programs are affected by such a change? This type of cross-reference will be invaluable in the future.

9.5   LACK OF UNDERSTANDING

Can installation of a data dictionary improve documentation? Of course it can. Does improved documentation automatically follow from installation of a data dictionary? What do you think?

We've already noted that one of the big problems in the dictionary world is that people frequently don't like to do the work of keeping the dictionary up to date. What can be done about this?

Can dictionary reports be designed to really help the people who could use the information? Remember, the analysts and programmers are the users of this system. Information Center clients are also potential users. So are managers and business analysts.

Can the procedures for maintaining the dictionary become an integral part of the systems development process, or must they represent extra work?

Do the people who must provide the data or metadata receive fair value in return for their effort?

Who in your organization can review or audit dictionary maintenance to ensure that metadata is up to date, consistent, correct, and in accord with standards? The auditor must be competent and accepted.

9.6 LACK OF GOOD DATA

Obviously, the mere installation of a data dictionary isn't going to solve all of our data quality problems. Are there any ways we can use the dictionary here?

We've already discussed including data validation rules as a part of the data definitions in the dictionary. We must know what constitutes quality data before we can do very much to obtain it. If we know the validation rules, we can include them in appropriate data entry programs. To do this, we need to know which are the entry programs for particular data items, don't we?

Frequently, bad data is caused by the suppliers of the data. Can the dictionary tell us who these folks are?

Each of the preceding questions and observations involves several distinct issues, by the way. Here are some of them:

Have we designed an implementation that can contain the information?

Have we established appropriate procedures to ensure that the information will be placed in the dictionary?

Can the people who are supposed to keep the dictionary up to date obtain the information? This issue is neither silly nor trivial.

Does our dictionary document the business processes and procedures that furnish and validate the data? The questions asked above apply here, also.

9.7   DATA BASE

The only observation we'll make here is that accessibility is one of the key attributes of a data base. A good data dictionary implementation can make the difference between a miscellaneous collection of data and a usable data base.

9.8   DATA BASE MANAGEMENT SYSTEMS AND FOURTH GENERATION TOOLS

As we've seen, a dictionary or directory is an integral component of most data base management systems and fourth generation tools. It is very difficult, if not impossible, to make use of the report writers, query facilities, and application generators without an adequate data dictionary.

We've also noted already that without data administration and a sound data dictionary, the use of fourth generation systems can lead to a proliferation of independent systems and applications, which compounds all of our data-related problems.

9.9 REUSABLE CODE

Reusable code isn't really reusable if it is not well document-ed. This documentation doesn't have to be in a data dictionary, but why not put it there? Shouldn't we really keep a cross-reference between each reusable module and all of its uses? Suppose we find a mistake in a module? Or suppose we are considering a change to some module? When we do change one, should we recompile or relink all the programs that contain it? Some highly active data dictionaries can contain the actual module and keep the cross-reference automatically based on copy or call statements in the programs.

9.10 INFORMATION CENTERS, PERSONAL COMPUTERS, AND DECISION SUPPORT SYSTEMS

One of the biggest stumbling blocks in the implementation of these concepts lies in the need to extract the data from the processing systems. We can't extract it if we can't find it and understand what it really means. Frequently, this isn't easy. Can an accurate data dictionary help? To answer that question, ask yourself these additional questions:

How good are the software tools if the data is inaccurate?

Does the Information Center user know where the data comes from?

Does he or she know how current it is?

How much trouble will we encounter in establishing procedures to ensure that the user's data is updated when the data in the production system is updated?

Will we even have a record of the end user data bases that have been created via extractions from production data? How will we know who is affected by a change to a production system?

9.11 DESIGN METHODOLOGIES

The major design methodologies require collection and indexing of a lot of information about user requirements, reports, procedures, data elements, and the like. Would it make sense to keep this in a data dictionary? What would it take to do this?

If use of the dictionary were really a part of the design process and the dictionary reports really helped the designers, would this provide a motive for keeping the dictionary up to date? Would that help with the other things we've been discussing?

9.12 DATA MODELS, DATA BASE DESIGN, AND DATA ARCHITECTURES

Do these activities require the collection and manipulation of a lot of data, or should we say metadata? Doesn't everything in the immediately preceding section apply here, as well?

9.13 DATA BASE ADMINISTRATION AND DATA ADMINISTRATION

It is difficult to imagine effective data and data base administration without a sound dictionary implementation.

9.14 PACKAGES

Does the installation of purchased packages solve or compound the data-related problems we've discussed?

Do we need a way to inventory and cross-reference the data processed by the purchased packages? Does a given package contain its own dictionary? If so, is the dictionary compatible? Can we automate a process for extracting the necessary metadata from the package's dictionary and the process of updating our master dictionary? Are naming standards compatible? Can we resolve discrepancies via prefixing or suffixing? Does the vendor's documentation provide the information we need? If not, can we obtain it?

Can our data dictionary help here? Are there any special problems?

9.15 A FEW WORDS OF CAUTION

This chapter has indicated many possible extensions to the dictionary design contained in Chapter 7. In the next chapter we'll be looking more closely at some of these and also at some other possibilities. As we do so, keep this in mind: *it is unlikely that any enterprise is capable of implementing the most complete possible data dictionary in one big piece.* You should view this as a menu from which you can select the options with the greatest potential benefit for your installation. You can also keep in mind that you might want to add some of these extensions later. If you have considered this in your initial design, later phases may be easier. If no consideration was given at the outset, later phases may not be possible.

NOTES

1. This may sound silly or idealistic, but unfortunately we all too often embark on a major undertaking with no clear idea of why we are doing it, what we hope to accomplish, or how to measure success.

10 Extensions—and a Little Blue Sky

10.1 GENERAL COMMENTS

Up to this point, the data dictionary uses that have been discussed in any amount of detail have been relatively conservative. Figure 10.1 is another copy of the data model for the implementation we discussed in Chapter 7. You might not arrive at exactly the same configuration for your shop, but this is about the minimum that is worth the effort you will be putting into installing a data dictionary. Now we are going to look at possible extensions of this design. They will be based on the expanded list of objectives shown in Figure 10.2. (This repeats part of Figure 8.5.) Some of the ideas presented in this figure follow from the things we've already talked about. Some of them may not be as obvious. Most of them have been implemented somewhere.[1]

You should think of this chapter as a menu or an ideabook. It is very unlikely that any one installation will ever implement

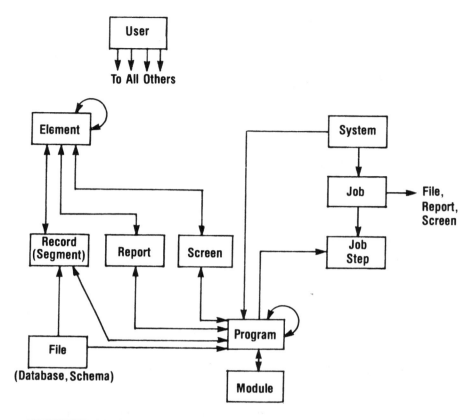

FIGURE 10.1 Conceptual Model of a Simple Dictionary

all of these extensions. You will probably find that you already are running some other pieces of software to keep track of some of the things discussed here.[2]

As you review the material in this chapter, it is very important that you keep in mind that actually doing some of these things is considerably more involved than you might think. In each case, you must:

Review the data model provided here;

Determine the changes necessary to make it appropriate for the way you do things at your shop;

Document Sources and Uses of Data

Support Data Model

Support Information Center

Support Application Generator

Support Life Cycle Methodology

Support Distributed Processing

Document Communications Network

Maintain Hardware Inventory

FIGURE 10.2   Additional Objectives

Determine how your organization would make use of the metadata;

Determine whether it is feasible to capture the metadata in your environment;

Identify the value of potential benefits and weigh it against the costs of implementation and maintenance;

Devise an appropriate implementation technique utilizing the extensibility features of your data dictionary;

Design appropriate procedures for obtaining the data and entering it;

Gain acceptance from those who must enter the data;

Devise appropriate input and output forms;

Evaluate the impact on your hardware environment;

Develop appropriate operating procedures;

Implement the features;

Allocate any additional disk space needed; and convert the data.

Implementing the necessary reports is a particularly important activity. You can be almost certain that it will be necessary to program custom reports, and thus to have a clear understanding of the requirement and of the internal structure of the dictionary data base. And keep in mind the possible impact of a major revision to the dictionary product on an organization with a large library of custom reports.

Also keep in mind that if a relatively large shop did implement everything in this chapter, it would require all of a large mainframe to operate the dictionary.

Make sure that you have a way to obtain accurate and timely updates for anything you design into your dictionary system. If data does not get updated it will be inaccurate, and any inaccuracy will destroy the credibility of the entire dictionary.

It isn't possible for this book to contain estimates of the work necessary to implement any of these suggestions. Too much depends on your environment, your skills, and how much you are already doing with your dictionary.

The method of this chapter is to go down the list of extensions, briefly explain the issues or problems, provide a very simple data model of the relevant entities and relationships, and briefly discuss implementation considerations.

As is the case throughout this book, each data model is a very simple entity relationship diagram. Each rectangle represents a data entity. Each line represents a relationship. An arrowhead represents the "many" side of a "one to many" or "many to many" relationship.[3]

10.2 DOCUMENT SOURCES AND USES OF DATA

In order to:

> evaluate the impact of system changes,
>
> make sound decisions as to which data is or is not sharable,
>
> implement appropriate data security procedures,
>
> or address data quality problems,

you must know where the data comes from and how it is used. That seems obvious, but you might be surprised to learn how hard that information is to obtain in some large organizations. This is particularly true for so-called mature systems that have survived organizational changes. There may be no one who recalls the original purpose of a report. The report may now be used for some purpose quite different from its original one. The original source of data may no longer exist. Very elaborate, but informal and undocumented, end user procedures may surround a particular report, screen, or input transaction.

Figure 10.3 is a simple diagram of relevant entities and relationships. Let's examine each one.

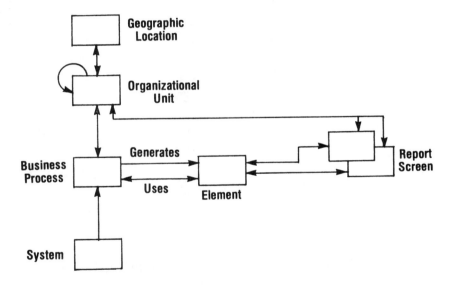

FIGURE 10.3   Sources and Uses of Data

GEOGRAPHIC LOCATION represents a physical location such as a plant or sales office. Possible attributes or descriptors include name, address, and type of facility.

ORGANIZATIONAL UNIT represents an appropriate subdivision of the organization such as a division or department. Which organizational units are appropriate? How is your company or enterprise organized? Descriptive attributes include name, identifying number or code, unit type, telephone number, and title of responsible person. Usually it isn't a good idea to include a person's name with this type of information because it can be very difficult to keep the data current.

BUSINESS PROCESS represents a particular activity or function of the enterprise which generates or uses the data. This could be something very generic like "inventory maintenance" or it could be very specific like "record receipt of shipment." How detailed should you make this? How good is the available information? How much work is the organization willing to do to keep it up to date? Will anyone be able to make use of detailed information? Notice that if use of the dictionary becomes an integral part of the development process, this information will be collected more or less automatically.

SYSTEM, DATA ELEMENT, REPORT, and SCREEN are discussed in Chapter 7. Notice that for this purpose we might concern ourselves with classes or groups of elements, or we might look at the most basic type of element.

The relationship between GEOGRAPHIC LOCATION and ORGANIZATIONAL UNIT is potentially a many to many relationship. A division might encompass several geographic locations. A plant might house several organizational units.

The relationship between ORGANIZATIONAL UNIT and BUSINESS PROCESS is also many to many.

The relationship between ORGANIZATIONAL UNIT and REPORT or SCREEN is also many to many.

There are at least two possible relationships between BUSINESS PROCESS and DATA ELEMENT. The process might create the element or it might make use of it. You should be asking yourself if you will really get enough benefit from this relationship to justify the effort of maintaining it. Relating either the ORGANIZATIONAL UNIT or the BUSINESS PROCESS to the REPORT or SCREEN might be good enough. And that might be hard enough to keep up.

One SYSTEM will generally be related to many BUSINESS PROCESSES.

You might implement GEOGRAPHIC LOCATION, ORGANI-ZATIONAL UNIT, and BUSINESS PROCESS as new entity types within the dictionary. A very reasonable alternative would be to make use of the USER entity that already exists in most dictionaries. It would then be necessary to add an attribute or classification to clearly and uniquely identify these special types of USERs. The advantage of this technique is that not only the entities but also appropriate relationships already exist in most dictionaries. It might be possible to make use of existing reports and screens, or it might be possible for you to make slight modifications to existing facilities rather than create brand new ones. This would not only save some work, it would also insulate you from possible future changes to the structure of the dictionary data base.

The big questions related to sources and uses of data have to do with getting and maintaining the information.

Someone in your data processing organization probably already maintains a distribution list for reports. There may also be a list of people to notify, given a problem with a particular system or delay in producing a report. There may be an inventory of terminals relating to geographic locations and users.

The communications software may contain tables relating users and/or passwords to specific systems and transactions.

The accounting and facilities management departments probably have lists of geographic locations, organizational units, and responsibilities.

All of these lists may be manually maintained or they may be produced from files or data bases. If the latter, they might be on mainframe systems or on floppy disks for processing by personal computers.

Discrepancies and inconsistencies are very likely to exist between different lists and files. These must be explored and resolved.

Can you devise reports that will be useful to the folks who have been keeping some of these lists? Can you implement update procedures that they will find friendlier that the procedures they currently employ? If so, they may be willing to provide the data necessary for maintaining this structure. Remember, the best possible motive someone could have for providing the information is that he or she gets something useful in return. This is much more effective than coercion could ever be. If a small change, or even a big change, in the report format that you just designed will obtain the cooperation you need, make the change!

10.3 SUPPORT DATA MODEL

The term data model can mean very different things to different people. Chapter 2 discusses most of the possibilities. The discussion here revolves around a very simple entity relationship type of model. The paper by Sakamoto and Ball (see note 1) discusses the implementation of a different type of model based on the IBM Business Systems Planning technique.

Figure 10.4 is a diagram of a simple data model. If you like the terminology, you can call it a *metamodel.*

BUSINESS PROCESS is discussed in the preceding section.

DATA ELEMENT is discussed in Chapter 7.

ENTITY represents a business entity, meaning just about any "thing" or concept you can identify that has relevance

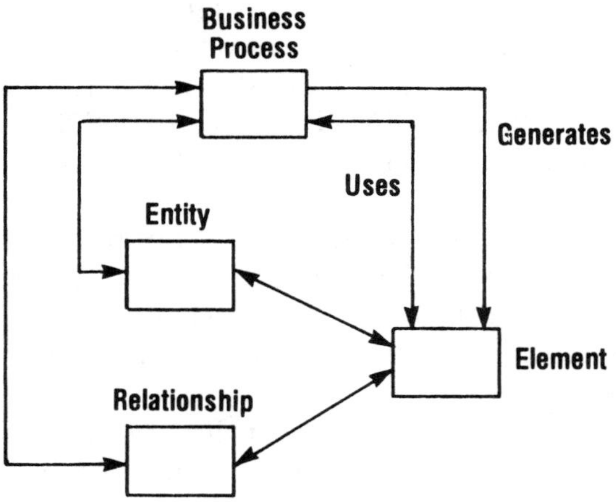

FIGURE 10.4   Diagram of a Simple Data Model

to the operation of your business or enterprise. That isn't a very good definition. It has been left vague intentionally. If you become serious about data modelling, you will have to expend some time and effort researching the topic, selecting a specific modelling technique, and learning that technique. In the process, you will acquire your specific definition of entity. The attributes or descriptors of ENTITY include a name and a definition.

RELATIONSHIP represents an association or connection between ENTITIES. The attributes of RELATIONSHIP also include name and definition.

The BUSINESS PROCESS to ENTITY relationship is many to many.

The BUSINESS PROCESS to RELATIONSHIP relationship is also many to many.

Most modelling techniques use the notion that two ENTITIES participate in any given RELATIONSHIP, while an ENTITY may participate in any number of RELATIONSHIPs.

The ENTITY to ELEMENT relationship and the RELA-
TIONSHIP to ELEMENT relationship are both potentially
many to many. Several ELEMENTs might describe a given
ENTITY or RELATIONSHIP. One ELEMENT might relate to
more than one ENTITY or RELATIONSHIP.

ENTITY and RELATIONSHIP could be represented by new
types of dictionary entities created via extensibility, or they
could be represented by the RECORD entity. The advantages
and disadvantages are the same as those discussed in the
preceding section.

As a rule, this type of entity relationship model is
represented by a diagram. Including this data in the dictionary
supplements the diagram; it does not do away with it. It is a
convenient way to document which ELEMENTs go with which
ENTITIES. Extensions are possible to document which RE-
CORDs, DATA BASEs, and FILEs contain information about
particular ENTITIES and RELATIONSHIPs and which SYSTEMs
and PROGRAMs support or perform which BUSINESS PROC-
ESSes. This type of information has great potential value, but *it
is also very difficult to compile and maintain.*

We've already noted that there is great variability in
modelling techniques and their use. The discussion must either
end here or go on at great length. Having indicated the
potential of the dictionary, it will stop here.

10.4   SUPPORT INFORMATION CENTER

The discussion that follows is as relevant for the end user with
a personal computer as for the user of an Information Center. It
would be too cumbersome to say "Information Center or
personal computer user" over and over, but please keep this
point in mind throughout the discussion.

There are actually two aspects to Information Center
support. One of these has already been addressed in the
preceding section and in Chapter 8. Information Center (and
personal computer) software has limited value without data.

Finding the required data for the Information Center is one of the biggest problems encountered by many organizations. The potential Information Center user has an interest in a given subject or in data about specific business entities and processes. The user may have no idea where the desired data is stored or may believe that the data resides in a particular system or that a copy of the data which appears on a particular report will meet his or her need. If the latter is the case, the user's belief may or may not be correct. In any event, the Information Center Analyst is expected to locate the required data, extract a copy from the appropriate files, and make it available for use.

Someone must discover that the data does, in fact, reside in certain files. Some form of data model, such as the one illustrated in Figure 10.4, would certainly help.

Accurate documentation of the content and arrangement of each type of record in each file or data base must exist. It is not at all unusual for the Information Center Analyst to be reduced to reading program code and deducing the record designs from the instructions in the programs. An even more insidious case is the one in which the documentation states that a certain data item appears in a certain location, and this is no longer true. Perhaps it never was true. The item may have been included for future expansion of the system, or, subsequent to file design, it may have become apparent that it was impossible to collect and maintain the data. It is even possible that data is present but is no longer maintained. Such things happen more often than you would like to believe. The older the program, the less reliable the documentation. Correct and up-to-date documentation in the form of the dictionary discussed in Chapter 7 would go a long way toward eliminating this type of problem.

After these problems have been resolved, a new set arises. The data must meet the user's time frame requirements. It may be necessary to provide the most current data possible at all times. Or the user's application may require that his or her copy remain static over an extended period of time. It may be necessary to provide data as of a specific date, such as the date of a month end closing.

Suppose a change is made that alters a file or data base design or alters the content of a data item. Will anyone advise the Information Center or the user? Will the people who make the change even know that the Information Center will be affected?

Suppose management or the auditors would like to keep track of who is obtaining copies of what data for security purposes. Can you be sure you know who the users of Information Center data files are? Can you be sure you know how the data is used? Can you be sure you know what additional copies are made using Information Center software?

Figure 10.5 illustrates some dictionary extensions that would resolve these issues. Let's look back at their characteristics.

GEOGRAPHIC LOCATION, ORGANIZATIONAL UNIT, DATA ELEMENT, RECORD, and FILE or DATA BASE are already old friends of ours.

INFORMATION CENTER FILE represents a data file for use on the Information Center (or on some personal computer). The naming convention and description must be appropriate to the hardware and software used. This could be the existing FILE entity, appropriately classified, or it could be a new type of dictionary entity. We've already discussed the relevant decision criteria.

Now, it becomes necessary to differentiate between a FILE and a DATA SET. This particular terminology is used in the IBM mainframe environment. The distinction always exists, but in some other environment different terminology may be used. Using this terminology, a FILE is more general than a DATA SET. A FILE is a pattern while a DATA SET is a specific occurrence. A payroll file for example is a description of the data used in payroll processing. A particular layout and type of data are associated with a particular FILE. A DATA SET is a specific occurrence of a FILE type, such as the version of the payroll file which was created on March 18, 1984. It is

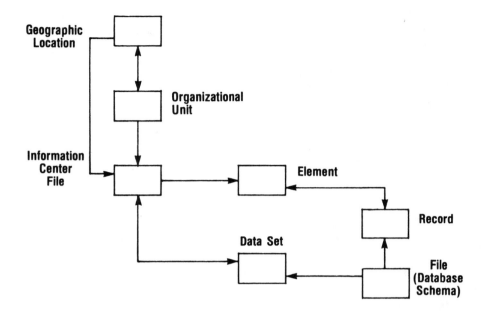

FIGURE 10.5   Information Center

normal for more than one DATA SET or version of a given
FILE to exist at the same time. They have unique DATA
SET names. It is also necessary to be sure you are using the
correct version. This is another case in which we might
create a new type of dictionary entity or make use of the
FILE entity. Frequently, information about DATA SETS
already exists in a system catalog, a tape library system, a
disk management system, a job scheduling system and
possibly several other places. It may not be desirable to add
yet another copy of the same data. It might be best to
document the required version as an attribute of the
INFORMATION CENTER FILE entity and let the other
software do the rest of the work. The other software
should, of course, be documented in some sort of metamodel.

The relationship between INFORMATION CENTER FILE
and DATA ELEMENT is potentially many to many.

One INFORMATION CENTER FILE can relate to several DATA SETS. A given DATA SET may also relate to more than one INFORMATION CENTER FILE.

The relationships between FILES and DATA SETS are one FILE to many DATA SETS.

Notice that since the USERS and the INFORMATION CENTER FILE may not be at the same GEOGRAPHIC LOCATION it is necessary to provide for the relationship of one GEOGRAPHIC LOCATION to many USERS and many FILES.

In most organizations, a given INFORMATION CENTER FILE will relate to only one ORGANIZATIONAL UNIT. You should verify that this is true for your organization.

In most organizations the data depicted in Figure 10.5 will be much easier to obtain than many of the other things we've discussed.

10.5 SUPPORT APPLICATION GENERATOR

For our purposes here, the term application generator refers to any of the wide variety of software packages that offer relief from conventional programming techniques. These are often called fourth generation tools. The basic concept of most available systems involves telling the computer "what is wanted" without having to tell it "how to go about it." This is the distinction between non-procedural and procedural systems.

The oldest non-procedural systems are probably the report program generator systems (RPG). These were used extensively twenty or more years ago, but then fell into disfavor in the large mainframe environment. Use of RPG is still common among users of intermediate-size computer systems such as the IBM System 36.

The typical RPG system contains standardized logic for producing reports. The user prepares specifications defining the appearance of the input, the appearance of the output, and the required calculations. The RPG system then processes these, producing the required report program as output. The output of older RPG systems was usually an assembly language source program which had to be processed by the assembler to produce a usable program. This two-phase process is somewhat cumbersome. Also, the required format of the specifications can be cryptic and confusing.

The capabilities of the older systems were somewhat limited, but for the right sort of application RPG can be a great time and labor saver. Many hours have probably been wasted writing programs in COBOL or Fortran or assembly language when they could have been created much more quickly via RPG. Some of the newer RPG systems are quite powerful and easy to use.

Another example is the report generator type of system. The earlier report generator systems used specification forms very similar to those used by RPG. The difference lies in the elimination of the intermediate program. Instead of producing a program, a report generator operates directly on the data, producing the desired report as a result. This is less cumbersome, but since the specifications must be reinterpreted each time a report is run, this type of system tends to be more expensive to operate because more machine resources are consumed.

It is a little amusing to note that both RPG systems and report generator systems (and also the report writer feature of the COBOL programming language) have been around quite a while, are true labor-saving tools, and have many of the capabilities of the very fashionable new fourth generation application-generating tools, but they never really caught on.

What do the new systems provide that the older ones do not?

Some provide a wider variety of operations and make it possible to create not only more sophisticated reports but also update programs.

Many are oriented toward on-line systems.

Many of the on-line products allow the user to specify the appearance of the input and output formats by examples— that is, by "painting them on the terminal."

Many of them contain, or are integrated with, some form of data base management system.

Many of them contain, or are integrated with, some form of data dictionary or directory.

The last item on the list is not only the most important from the standpoint of this book, it is also the most important in terms of adding capability to a system. Once a data element has been defined to the system in terms of size, type, validation, editing, and storage location, it need not be redefined every time a new report is desired.[4]

Our modern application generators have tremendous potential as labor-saving tools if they are understood for what they are and used with great care. For example, small free-standing reporting systems can be created more quickly than would be possible if conventional programming techniques were used. However, the implementer must still define the data elements correctly, must find a way to obtain the data elements (either by creating a brand new file of data or by extracting the data from existing files), *and must gain an understanding of the reporting requirements and the data before starting.*

Reports and extracts of data from existing files and data bases can be created easily using application generators *if the data elements are well documented in the data dictionary.* It must be possible to determine that a given data element name does, in fact, represent the desired data element. The format can be "painted on the screen" only if the data dictionary does contain proper editing rules. Updates can be created only if the data dictionary does contain correct and complete validation rules for the data elements. And, it is necessary to assess the impact on the environment. How will the new application interact with existing applications which already use the data elements? Will there be data consistency problems? Will data security constraints be violated? Will performance or capacity problems be created?

Figure 10.6 shows dictionary entities and extensions that are relevant to application generators.

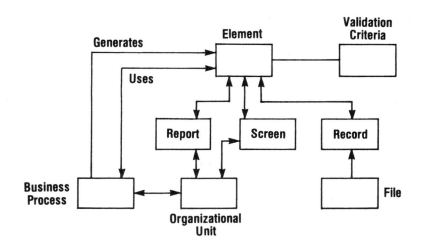

FIGURE 10.6   Application Generator

DATA ELEMENT is discussed in several other places in this book. Here, it is essential to note that effective use of the new software tools requires that editing rules, validation rules, security rules, and a good definition be contained in the dictionary. (If the generator does not use the organization's primary data dictionary, it is necessary to provide some mechanism for extracting this information and making it available in the proper form.[4]

SCREEN, RECORD, REPORT, FILE, and BUSINESS PROCESS are also discussed elsewhere. At this point, let's just note that whatever we are making with our generator is another use of the DATA ELEMENT. Procedures for using the tool should ensure that this use will be documented.

10.6   SUPPORT LIFE CYCLE METHODOLOGY

There are two main aspects to life cycle support. First, most methodologies call for the collection and analysis of a lot of data. (Actually, a lot of it is really metadata, isn't it?) The data dictionary can be used to mechanize some of this. Second, integration of the dictionary with the methodology *can* result in nearly automatic dictionary maintenance. The word *can* is italicized here because it takes a lot of planning, preparation, and selling to make this a reality. You will achieve this only if dictionary update procedures do harmonize with the methodology, and if the system developers really do find the dictionary reports and queries useful. If you merely issue an edict that says, "You will provide the data dictionary administration group with the following . . . ', chances are good that the only thing you will get is an argument.

Thus, it is essential that you study your organization's methodology and its use of the methodology carefully, identify appropriate points of intersection, develop useful reports, and, above all, solicit participation of the systems development group in developing the procedures and formats.

Some life cycle methodologies that are currently marketed already have interfaces with software tools that mechanize parts of the process. These must also be investigated. The discussion which follows can only be of a general nature because there are differences from product to product and also because many methodologies on the market are considered proprietary by their developers and dissemination of information is restricted.

There is yet another problem here. Most accepted data base design methodologies begin with the collection of data about data—data elements, entities, reports, and the like. Many system development methodologies begin with the study of processes and functions. The attempt to merge these two approaches can give rise to many interesting discussions (and possibly a fist fight or two). If you think about it, the two approaches do need to be merged. It is artificial to separate a process from the data it uses or to separate the data from the processes which use it.

With all that in mind, take a look at Figure 10.7. This illustrates the dictionary entities you would create for life cycle methodology support.

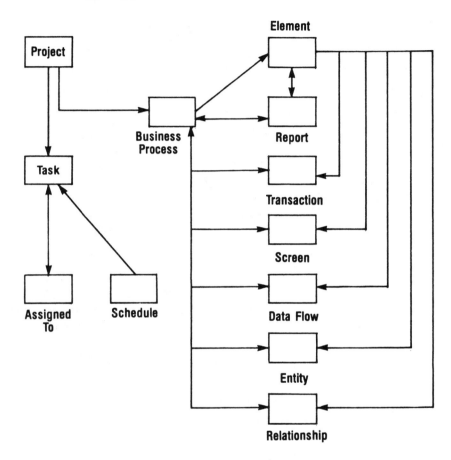

FIGURE 10.7   Life Cycle

DATA ELEMENT, REPORT, SCREEN, ENTITY, RELA-TIONSHIP, and BUSINESS PROCESS aren't new to us. It is worth noting that obtaining good definitions of these as the system is defined will not only improve documentation of the system, it will also improve the quality of the development effort.

PROJECT is used to tie together all items related to a specific project. It will be a new entity created via extensibility. Its attributes include name, sponsor, completion date, and priority.

OBJECTIVE refers to a specific goal to be achieved by the project. It will be a new entity created via extensibility. Attributes include name and description.

TASK represents a specific task to be performed in the process of developing the system. It will be a new entity created via extensibility. Attributes include name, description, and status.

ASSIGNED TO identifies a particular individual who will be assigned one or more tasks. This could be another disguise of our old friend, the USER, or it could be a new entity. I recommend taking advantage of USER because most dictionary systems already provide for relationships between USER and just about every other entity. Attributes include name and title.

SCHEDULE represents the milestone date to be associated with one or more tasks. It would be a new entity created via extensibility rather than an attribute of TASK, in order to simplify reporting. You might also make use of a classification device such as the Cullinet CLASS ATTRIBUTE structure.

DATAFLOW represents a collection of elements which passes from one process to another. It can effectively be represented by the RECORD entity.

One PROJECT will consist of many TASKs.

TASK to ASSIGNED TO is a many to many relationship.

SCHEDULE to TASK is one to many.

One PROJECT can relate to many BUSINESS PROCESSes. Is this correct? Could a single BUSINESS PROCESS relate to more than one PROJECT?

BUSINESS PROCESS has a many to many relationship with ELEMENT, REPORT, TRANSACTION, SCREEN, DATAFLOW, ENTITY, and RELATIONSHIP.

The other relationships are discussed in Chapter 7, in Section 10.2, and elsewhere.

The issue of multiple dictionaries is also relevant here. Many installations find it beneficial to separate production from development. There might be a single development dictionary, or a separate dictionary for each team. Make sure you've looked at operating costs and data migration before you get into this. Remember, you may need to provide developers with copies of the definitions that go with production systems— and someday the development system must migrate to production.

10.7 SUPPORT DISTRIBUTED PROCESSING

The availability of inexpensive processors (including personal computers) and advances in telecommunications technology have made distributed processing a fact of life for many organizations. Distributed processing does provide a cost-effective solution to many problems. It can also create a lot of problems. To be specific, it can be an administrative nightmare. We'll discuss hardware issues in the next two sections; here we'll just address actual system and processing issues.

Essentially, we can't administer the operation unless we know which JOBs are run at which GEOGRAPHIC LOCATIONs and when they are run.

Figure 10.8 illustrates some relevant entities and relationships.

GEOGRAPHIC LOCATION, FILE OR DATA BASE, SYSTEM, JOB, and JOBSTEP have already been discussed.

FEATURE OR PARAMETER refers to a system option that may not be used at all locations, or a parameter setting that

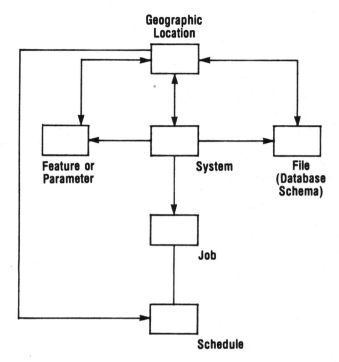

FIGURE 10.8   Distributed Processing

may vary from location to location. Attributes include name, definition, and explanation of all possible values. This is a new entity created via extensibility.

SCHEDULE represents the schedule for running the job. This will also be a new entity created via extensibility.

The relationships are not as straightforward as they first seem. A JOB may be run at a GEOGRAPHIC LOCATION that is remote from the FILE. Not all JOBSTEPS for a SYSTEM need to be run at all GEOGRAPHIC LOCATIONS. Why don't you review each relationship on your own and see what you come up with?

10.8   DOCUMENT COMMUNICATIONS NETWORK

Keeping track of the communications side of a large network is another big task. Figure 10.9 shows some of the relevant entities. Only one of these has been discussed in previous sections. Most will probably be new entities created via extensibility.

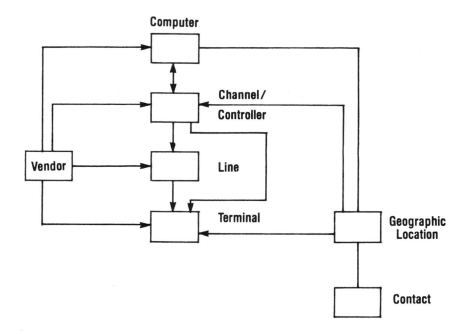

FIGURE 10.9   Communications Network

COMPUTER refers specifically to a central processor or CPU. Its attributes include identifier, name, model, number, and description.

CHANNEL or CONTROLLER has attributes similar to COMPUTER.

LINE represents a specific communications link. Attributes include identifier, quality, and speed.

TERMINAL has the same attributes as LINE. Note that it is necessary to make a decision here. Is a personal computer a terminal? It really isn't. That is fairly clear, but what about an automated teller machine or point of sale device? It might have as much local intelligence as a personal computer. Since neither of these is general in purpose, we'd best call them terminals.

GEOGRAPHIC LOCATION is not new to us.

CONTACT represents the person to contact regarding problems and outages. This could be another disguise for USER.

VENDOR is the corporation from which the hardware is purchased or leased.

You may find that most of this information is already maintained by some form of network management software. This type of software frequently operates on special hardware that is designed to monitor and control telecommunications activity.

10.9 MAINTAIN HARDWARE INVENTORY

This is a different aspect of the problem addressed in the two preceding sections. Figure 10.10 contains only one dictionary entity that we haven't already seen. SOFTWARE LICENSE represents a license to run a specific software product on a specific machine. The proliferation of hardware has made it necessary to keep track of this.

10.10 CONCLUDING REMARKS

It's worth repeating that no one organization is likely to implement all of the possibilities discussed in this chapter. On the other hand, there are still more possibilities—change and

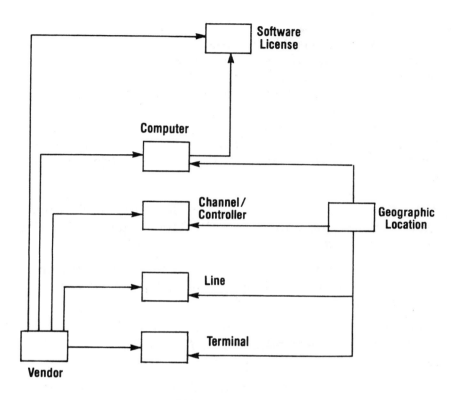

FIGURE 10.10   Hardware Inventory

problem control, for example. Our purpose has been to show that a data dictionary is a generalized data base system that can be used for tracking and reporting many kinds of metadata. If you decide to implement any of these, you should use the analysis given here as only a starting point. You absolutely need to spend time studying how your shop does things and develop an appropriate configuration to go with that. As we discuss in note 2, any data processing shop could benefit greatly from the exercise of studying the relevant data entities and determining where and how the metadata is currently stored. This study might well be worth more than any possible dictionary implementation.

NOTES

1. It may be impossible to avoid plagiarizing someone else's work in this chapter. We list a number of references here to provide blanket coverage, but it just is not possible to sort out specific references for every idea contained in this chapter. As a matter of fact, some of the things that the author thinks are original probably come from some presentation or paper that has been forgotten. Perhaps anyone not included on the list of references will be forgiving. Some of these references have already been cited in previous chapters.

Alif, Allan. *Automated Enterprise Modelling and Database Design*. Paper presented at IEEE Trends and Applications Conference, May 1984.

F. Allen, M. Loomis, and M. Manning. "The Integrated Dictionary/Directory System." *ACM Computing Surveys*. 14 (June 1982).

Armstrong Cork Co. "Data Management in a BSP Environment." Paper presented at DATAMANAGER User Meeting, 1979.

Cullinet Software, Inc. *Integrated Data Dictionary Methodologies: Classroom Aids*. Westwood, Mass.: Cullinet, 1982.

———. *Integrated Data Dictionary User's Guide*. Westwood, Mass.: Cullinet, 1982.

GUIDE. "Data Administration in a Distributed Data Environment." Paper, 1982.

———. "Data Administration Methodology." Working paper, 1978.

———. "Data Modelling Experience at Hobart Corporation." Paper presented at GUIDE Meeting, 1983.

———. "Dictionary Utilization an Hobart Corporation." Paper presented at GUIDE Meeting, 1981.

IBM Corporation. *An Architecture for Managing the Information Systems Business.* White Plains, N.Y.: IBM, 1980.

———. *DB/DC Data Dictionary: Applications Guide.* San Jose, Calif.: IBM, 1979.

———. *DB/DC Data Dictionary: User's Guide.* San Jose, Calif.: IBM, 1977.

———. *DB/DC Data Dictionary: Implementation Primer.* Santa Teresa, Calif.: IBM, 1979.

———. *DB/DC Data Dictionary Sample User Handbook.* Middlesex, England: IBM, 1983.

———. *Information Systems Planning Guide.* White Plains, N.Y.: IBM, 1981.

S. Iyers and A. Wilson. *A Dictionary Driven Development Methodology.* Paper presented at IEEE Trends and Applications Conference, May 1984.

Leong-Hong and B. Plagman. *Data Dictionary/Directory Systems: Administration, Implementation and Usage.* New York: John Wiley & Sons, 1982.

Management Systems and Programming, Inc. *The Data Dictionary in Systems Development.* Lexington, Mass.: MSP, 1980.

J. Martin. *Strategic Data-Planning Methodologies.* Englewood Cliffs, N.J.: Prentice-Hall, 1982.

Provident National Bank. *System Development Methodology.* Philadelphia, Pa.: Private communication, 1980.

R. Ross. *Data Dictionaries & Data Administration.* New York: AMACOM, 1981.

Royal Bank of Canada. *O & S Data Dictionary Standards and Techniques.* Toronto: Private communication, 1981.

J. G. Sakamoto and F. W. Ball. "Supporting Business Systems Planning Studies with the DB/DC Data Dictionary." *IBM Systems Journal* 21 (1982).

Skandia Corporation. *Using the Dictionary to Support Systems Analysis.* New York: GUIDE Presentation, 1981.

J. Van Duyn. *Developing a Data Dictionary System.* Englewood Cliffs, N.J.: Prentice-Hall, 1982.

M. Walsh. *Database & Data Communications Systems: A Guide for Managers.* Reston, Va.: Reston Publishing, 1983.

2. Remember, the data dictionary is really a data base of data about data (or, if you prefer, metadata). Potential users of the dictionary include everyone interested in the enterprise's data. But, the data processing staff is the primary user. And, just as we developed applications for end users in a piecemeal and fragmented manner, we did the same thing for (or to) ourselves. In or around the typical large data processing installation, you will most likely find:

- a data base management system or two,
- a data dictionary,
- a source program library system,
- possibly, an additional library system for job control,
- a tape library system,
- disk space management software,
- a project management and scheduling system,
- a production job scheduling system,
- a time recording system,
- a problem tracking system,
- a job accounting system,
- a hardware inventory system,
- a system for managing the communications network

- several personal computers running various spreadsheets and "databases"

- and a lot of other things.

Frequently these will be purchased packages. Those purchased from the same vendor may share data. In today's environment, any two packages that can even pass data files back and forth are called "integrated systems." Generally speaking, the redundancies, inconsistencies, and inaccuracies will match anything the end users have.

Just as it is not practical to consider redoing all the business applications, it isn't practical to think about scrapping all the software on this list and doing it all with a data dictionary. It would just be too much work. There are people with vested interests in the way things are presently done. In some cases, people aren't quite sure what the existing software does or how it does it.

But, it is food for thought. In any large shop, and probably any small one too, there is a lot of room for improvement. This chapter provides some ideas about things that can be done. Just tracking down what is stored and where it is stored would be beneficial in most places.

A very worthwhile project would be to develop your technique for data modelling using the data dictionary, try it out on the data center entities, and then document which attributes of which entities are stored in each software package. This would provide an opportunity to refine the technique. It would also produce a valuable end product.

3. The many to many relationship usually causes problems when it comes to implementation. Most data base management systems and most data dictionaries provide ways to create only one to one and one to many relationships. The usual solution is to create an extra object (a pseudo-entity?) to stand for the relationship. Figure 10.11 illustrates this point. If you examine the internals of your dictionary, you will find that it does contain this sort of thing for standard many to many relationships. If you add new many to many relationships, you will have to create these extra entities yourself.

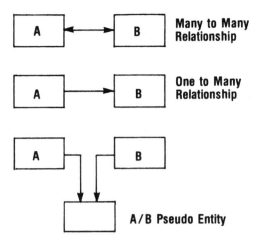

FIGURE 10.11 Many to Many

4. Back in the dark ages of punched cards, any smart programmer had a drawer full of card decks containing definitions of commonly used data files. Those who worked with RPG or a report generator naturally had these in the form required for the generator. To a certain extent, our modern data dictionaries are merely extensions of this time-honored device.

It is becoming very common for program-generating or application-generating systems to contain data dictionaries or directories. You are likely to find yourself confronted with multiple dictionary/directory systems. Each will have its own unique set of data entities and its own form of data dictionary definition language. The only way you could possibly avoid this would be to buy all software from the same vendor. This might not be possible—and in some cases, you would still have the problem.

What is the solution? Consider one dictionary to be the master. Use the dictionary reporting facility or a custom program to extract metadata in the proper format for updating each subsidiary dictionary. Institute procedures which ensure that all dictionary updates are performed via the master dictionary.

11 Recipe Book (or Menu?)

11.1 INTRODUCTION

This chapter is an attempt to pull together everything we've discussed so far. The word attempt is used because it may be impossible to do that. A work which really did bring it all together would rival the *Encyclopedia Brittanica*.

You would probably like a cookbook containing precise instructions for a successful data dictionary implementation. We've noted before that there are many variables and that there are significant differences between organizations. The best we can hope for is some combination of an outline, a checklist, and a discussion of key issues and choices.

Actually, you might consider this chapter a combination of a menu and a recipe book. It contains many suggestions and many questions you must somehow answer. You should find that the answers to the questions will lead you to specific plans and actions. If you can't answer the questions, you'd best look harder for the answers. You are bound to have trouble later if you proceed without knowing what you are doing. At minimum, you should keep a written record of each question and answer. You should also keep track of how each answer was obtained. You will have to be the one to decide exactly how each item applies to your situation.

It is a good idea to read more than one book on the subject of data dictionaries and data administration before you plunge into this activity. Durrell[1] and Ross[2] will be particularly valuable. There are many others you might also look at. The "catchall" list of references given in note 1 for Chapter 10 contains many good suggestions.

A main premise of this chapter, and really of this entire book, is that the installation of a Data Dictionary involves a lot more than the technical implementation of a piece of software. It really constitutes the creation of a system for the management of data about data—metadata. The implications of this are far-reaching. A successful implementation will radically alter the process of designing, developing, implementing, using, and maintaining information systems in your organization. It is also likely to change the way the entire enterprise operates. If the change is for the better, the project can be considered a genuine success. A failure will either have no impact or will change things for the worse. Most likely, a failure will create a lot of "busy work" and a lot of hard feelings.

The conclusion that follows from this is that you should analyze and design for a data dictionary system in the same way you would analyze and design for the implementation of any major system. If you use a formal methodology for the design and implementation of business systems, you should use it here also. If you have no methodology, by the way, you will probably have a lot of trouble doing very much with a data dictionary.

The organization of this chapter reflects the simplified life cycle introduced in section 8.3.3, The Elements of a Plan. That material is more fully developed here. In some cases, material from preceding chapters is repeated here. Once again, you should use this material as an adjunct to your particular development methodology.

Naturally, you should document and present your findings in an appropriate manner that is consistent with your current practice. If you do not have a satisfactory current practice, you might follow any standard text of systems development—Senn, for example.[3]

You should continually ask yourself if you believe the statements and assertions that are made here. Honesty demands a frank admission that many of them cannot be proven. Most represent common sense; most are in accord with contemporary thinking on systems development and planning. But, it is very difficult, if not impossible, to compile statistics that will prove, beyond doubt, the value of a particular approach. So, it is not only valid, it is also necessary for you to analyze and question each recommendation.

11.2   GETTING STARTED

11.2.1   Setting Objectives

You'd best start by asking a number of basic questions.

Who has initiated this project?

Why has it been initiated?

What goals are to be achieved?

What problems are to be solved?

Who are the prospective users of a data dictionary? Possibilities include programmers, systems analysts, computer operations personnel, data processing planners, data processing managers, end users of information, managers, and others.

Who must participate in the implementation?

Who must cooperate?

What approvals and authorization are needed?

It will be necessary to keep going back to these questions at each stage of development. As you learn more about your organization and your problems, your answers to some of these questions are likely to change.

If you are the one who is initiating the activity, your first order of business is to determine who must be convinced and what sorts of arguments are most likely to convince them. That really means you must find out how you can help them. Chapters 1, 2, and 9 of this book contain material that is useful here. Typical data processing problems, possible solutions, and the relevance of a data dictionary to these are discussed. Section 8.3.1, Support and Commitment are Needed, and section 8.3.2, How to Justify a Dictionary, are also highly relevant.

At the risk of some redundancy, let's just list the problems from Chapter 1 and the typical solutions from Chapter 2. This will help focus our thinking.

The problems we've reviewed in Chapter 1 are: redundant data, redundant processing, complexity and interdependence, difficulty of change, lack of adequate documentation, inconsistent data, inconsistent representations and codes, inconsistent timing, lack of understanding, lack of good data, and lack of organization.

The potential solutions we've discussed are: data base, data base management systems, data dictionaries, fourth generation tools and prototyping, reusable code, information centers, personal computers, decision support systems, design methodologies, data models, data base design methodologies, data architectures, data base administration and data administration, and purchased packages.

Any discussion of any solution to any of the problems we've listed will revolve around one of two possibilities: a software solution or a solution that involves administration and managing data. Do you believe pure software solutions really exist?

Your problem will be to explain or demonstrate that careful management of data is a key component of any solution and that careful management of data can be facilitated by a dictionary. The specific justifications contained in section

8.3.2, subsections Cost, Enhanced Capability, and How Then to Justify a Dictionary are based on this premise.

You have to tailor the presentation of this material to a particular audience. Most managers are not interested in a lot of detail about data elements, files, jobstreams, and the like. Nor do they like to hear a lot of jargon and buzzwords. They do want to hear how your proposal will solve specific problems that they perceive or further specific goals that they have formulated.

Typical executive concerns regarding data processing, as identified by Dennis Severance of the University of Michigan Business School,[4] include

Erosion of position through computer systems obsolescence

Inefficient use of computer resources

Excessive computer expenditures

Unresponsive information system function

Dissipation of management energy

Interruption of business activities

Destruction of accounting or control records

Material inaccuracies in accounting or control records

Manipulation of accounting or control records, and

Exposure of sensitive corporate information

Technically oriented people, on the other hand, might demand very specific illustrations and examples.

11.2.2 Determining Project Scope

It will be well worth your while to spend some time at the outset determining what you believe you are to accomplish, who must be convinced, and what are the most promising arguments. It is also necessary to determine exactly what is being proposed. Is it the purchase and installation of a data dictionary? Is it the implementation of data administration? Is it the initiation of strategic data planning and corporate information resource management?

How broad are your ambitions? Section 7.2, Specific Objectives, lists some very specific and limited objectives. These are restricted to the resolution of problems within the data processing organization. Let's repeat them here.

Standardize the names, definitions, and physical descriptions of the data elements used in all programs. Standardize the column headings used on reports and the labels used on display formats.

Document which data is kept in which files or databases or schemas.

Document which programs, jobs, and systems access and update which data elements in which files or databases or schemas.

Document which reports and screens are produced by which programs, jobs, and systems.

Document which modules and subprograms are included in which programs.

Document processing schedules, file back-up and retention, and responsibilities for program and jobstream maintenance.

Chapter 10 suggests a number of more ambitious objectives: document sources and uses of data, support data model, support information center, support application generator, support life cycle methodology, support distributed processing, document communications network, and maintain hardware inventory.

Notice that in section 7.3, Assumptions, we addressed the environment. You might review the assumptions we made there and note whether or not they are appropriate in your situation. Let's repeat them here.

A data base administration or data dictionary administration group exists and has been formally charged with installing and maintaining a data dictionary.

There is a desire and willingness to standardize naming conventions and procedures in our data processing shop.

It will be possible to obtain good data element, transaction, and system definitions for new and existing systems.

We have or can obtain good documentation of our existing data elements, files, modules, subprograms, programs, copy libraries, load libraries, job control language files, systems, etc.

We have a well-defined concept of what a system is. We know which systems we have.

We are not doing data administration for the entire organization right now.

There are a number of fairly obvious questions you can ask at this point.

Does a data base administration function already exist in your organization? Is it effective?

If there is no data base administrator, why is this so? If a current data base administrator is ineffective, why is this so?

Do good standards and procedures already exist? If not, why not? Are standards and procedures adhered to? Why? Why not?

Is there a development methodology? Is it consistently followed? Why? Why not?

Is there a commitment to long-range planning for data processing? If not, why not? What plans exist? Have plans been followed? Why? Why not? A long-range plan should include (1) an overall information system architecture, (2) identification of a portfolio of applications that will provide complete coverage of needs, (3) identification of clear boundaries between applications, (4) a plan for orderly development of applications, based on priorities and the requisite physical development sequence, and (5) data requirements for shared data bases.[5]

Is there a commitment to long-range planning for the enterprise? If not, why not? What plans exist? Have plans been followed? Why? Why not? Are plans disrupted by forces within the enterprise or by forces beyond the enterprise's control?

Has any sort of data model, data architecture, information architecture, or business planning model been proposed? Has the activity been carried out? Was it productive? Why? Why not?

How fragmented is the data processing organization? Do different groups communicate and cooperate? Why? Why not?

How fragmented is the enterprise? Do different groups communicate and cooperate? Why? Why not?

Is data processing geographically dispersed?

Is the enterprise geographically dispersed? How readily can you determine which data is actually used at which location?

What component or sector of the enterprise can you realistically hope to address?

If you address each of these questions and obtain accurate answers for most of them, you will automatically begin to understand what is a realistic project and what is not. You will also begin to see who must be convinced and how difficult it might be. You will also want to review these questions at each stage to determine whether or not the original answers still seem valid.

If the answers to many of these questions are no, you may be tempted to assume a "savior" role and attempt to solve all the problems. Things will be a lot better if you set realistic objectives.

There are two key ingredients for a successful project: commitment and realistic goals. Current wisdom has it that *you cannot effect true data resource management without participation and commitment from end users and management.* This conclusion is based on observations of many failures. It appears to be valid. Review in section 8.3.1 the subsections Management Commitment and Is Management Commitment Enough for more discussion of this.

Many, many failures have resulted from a plan that was too ambitious and a gross underestimate of the effort involved. Be careful. Be sure you have really evaluated the effort required to implement your plan. Be sure to consider organizational impacts.

11.2.3 Preliminary Study Report

At this point, you should prepare a preliminary study or proposal. The exact nature and form will be dictated by your particular situation. It should document the research you have conducted, the answers to the questions, the objectives you will achieve, the costs and benefits, and the course of action to be followed. If possible, within the constraints imposed by the standards followed at your organization, the document should begin with a management summary that discusses these issues *clearly, briefly,* and *simply.*

The report should also contain a plan. This will, at minimum, indicate the next steps. It could outline the rest of the project. In the latter case, it should be made clear that the findings of subsequent, more detailed study may necessitate changes to the remainder of the plan. In fact, you can be nearly certain that this will happen. Most comprehensive methodologies provide for reevaluation of the overall plan at the end of each major phase. It is very unrealistic to ignore this necessity.

You will, of course, have had the benefit of reviewing the rest of this chapter and will incorporate the steps that follow into the plan.

11.2.4   Assign Personnel and Initiate Detailed Study

The number of individuals assigned to the next phase will be determined by the size of the organization and the scope of the project. The availability of staff for this project may also be a factor in establishing the scope. In a large organization, it could easily take a single individual six months, a year, or more to conduct the research and develop a detailed plan.

Individuals assigned to this phase of the project should have keen analytical skills. They should have a knowledge of the organization and its workings. Interpersonal and communication skills are also very important. They should have enough technical knowledge to be able to review documentation and discuss technical issues intelligently. *The analytical skills, knowledge of the organization, and interpersonal skills are much more important than a great deal of technical expertise.*

The study to be conducted is the topic of the next section.

11.3   DETAILED STUDY

The exact steps of the study will be dictated by your specific objectives, your methodology, and the nature of your organization. Key elements are discussed below.

11.3.1   Identify Organizational Structure

It will be necessary to identify the information processing organization, the division of responsibilities, and the interfaces between organizational units. Here are the questions to ask.

What is the formal organization chart structure?

Is there an informal organization structure which super-cedes the formal structure?

What are the specific functions and duties of each organizational unit?

What is communicated from one unit to another? How is it communicated? Don't overlook casual and informal chan-nels. How effective is the communication? How well do different units cooperate?

11.3.2   Identify Existing Practices

Existing practices might be identified via personal knowledge, interviews, questionnaires, and observations. Be particularly careful about relying on personal observation, especially in a large organization. Are you sure everyone does things the way you think they do? Don't document what you do or what you think the others *should* do. Find out what is actually done.

Here are more questions. Your particular study may not require you to ask each of these questions. You'll have to review them and make your selections.

How are systems developed?

What are the processes and data flows of the system development and maintenance cycles?

How are end user needs communicated and analyzed?

How are needs evaluated?

What approvals are obtained?

How are data elements documented?

What naming standards exist? Are they consistently followed? If they are not followed, why is this so?

How are files and data bases designed and documented?

How are programs, jobstreams, and systems designed and documented? Is the documentation used? If it is not, what are the reasons?

How are projects and teams organized?

What reviews occur? Who conducts them?

How are program source statements and versions managed?

How are program source listings managed?

How are changes and problems tracked?

How are programs and systems validated and tested?

What are the procedures for migration of new systems from test to production status? Specifically ask about data flows, detailed procedures, documents, and checklists.

What are the procedures for migration of changes to existing systems from test to production status? Specifically ask about data flows, detailed procedures, documents, and checklists.

What operating guides exist? How are they developed and maintained? How are they distributed? Are they useful? Are they used? If not, why not?

How are reports distributed to users? How is this process documented?

Can you determine which program or system produces each report or screen? Can you do this without reference to the program documentation?

Can users of particular systems and reports be identified? How?

What data security procedures are in place? Who has the authority to authorize or refuse access to specific data items?

How is data security implemented for on-line applications?

How well are data terminal locations and access authorities documented? How are these controlled?

How are passwords and access authorizations assigned and controlled? Who does this? What records are kept?

Is there an Information Center? If so, how is data furnished to the Information Center? How are Information Center applications developed *and documented?* Are there formal procedures? What security procedures exist here?

How extensive is the use of personal computers? How is data furnished to the personal computers? How well is this documented and controlled? How are personal computer applications developed *and documented?* What security procedures are in place here?

Is processing distributed? How is this documented? What controls and security procedures exist? How was the partitioning of data and processing established?

In regard to each of the above, how consistent are the practices from one system to another or one organizational unit to another?

11.3.3 Review Existing Systems

It will be necessary to identify and enumerate existing systems. This may not be as easy as you think! Be sure to include systems used within the data processing department or group! See section 10.1, General Comments, section 10.4, Support Application Generator, section 10.6, Support Life Cycle Methodology, and section 10.7, Support Distributed Processing for some ideas on this.

Don't neglect software used to support data processing operations—source library systems, job scheduling systems, disk management systems, program generators, and the like.

Don't neglect your purchased software packages.

For each existing system you should identify the end users, number of programs, number of lines of code, number of files, number of record types, number of data element types, number of reports, number of screens, number of end users, volume of data, volume of transactions, and number of outstanding problems. You will learn a lot when you see whether or not you have trouble obtaining this information.

You should review documentation on a system-by-system basis to determine whether or not the answers to the questions in section 11.3.2 are consistent from one system to another. If they are not, you should document which systems adhere to which standards. It should be obvious that the more inconsistencies there are, the more problems you have to solve.

You should also be sure to determine which systems are currently being rewritten and which are scheduled for rewrite in the near future.

11.3.4   Review System Interfaces

At this point you need to address communication between different systems. You do not, however, want to identify and document each interface. That is something you'll do later. At this point, you are attempting to assess the ease with which this information can be obtained later on.

Here are the questions.

Does program and system documentation consistently address intersystem and interprogram data transfers and dependencies?

Does an overall systems architecture or integrated systems flow chart exist? If so, how is it maintained? Is it kept up to date? If it is not kept up to date, why is this so?

How extensive are intersystem data transfers?

How common are shared files and data bases?

What problems have been caused by misunderstandings regarding data transfers and shared files?

Are the end users aware of data transfers and shared files?

Do end user procedures provide for consistency and integrity? How well are they followed? If they are not followed, what is the reason?

You might want to think of Information Center and personal computer applications as having system interfaces. These frequently involve the extraction of data from production systems. They frequently require merging or sharing of data from several sources.

You should ask these questions.

How extensive is this practice?

How well is it documented?

Do the end users understand the data and its sources?

Do the developers of these applications experience problems in finding or extracting data? What sorts of problems do they experience?

11.3.5 Reevaluate Objectives

At this point you should have gathered and documented a lot of information about the way your organization processes and manages data, especially metadata. It is an appropriate time for reevaluation of the objectives you set when you addressed sections 11.2.1, Setting Objectives, and 11.2.2, Determining Project Scope. You would do well to review them one by one.

Does anything you've learned make you want to add or delete objectives?

Have you found any additional problems? Can you see how a data dictionary might help solve them?

How do you feel about the amount of effort required to implement your idea of a data dictionary?

Can you rank your revised list of objectives by importance?

Can you rank them according to the amount of effort required to achieve each one? Can you identify the amount of effort required to achieve each one? Might you consider eliminating the less beneficial or more difficult?

At this point, you might want to review your findings with your management or sponsor. This is an option you will have to evaluate in relation to your particular situation and your perception of management understanding and objectives. This could be a very informal review or it could involve a detailed report that documents the findings and suggests actions to be taken.

We'll assume an informal review. If you opt for a detailed report, you can use the content of section 11.6, Detailed Report and Plan, as a model.

11.3.6   A Logical Design for the Dictionary

Now you should be ready to develop a logical design for a dictionary that will meet the needs of your organization. In order to do this, you should relate your findings and objectives to your knowledge of data dictionaries.

Some of the preceding sections should be particularly useful. You might particularly like to review section 3.9, Dictionary Content; section 3.10, Extensibility; Chapter 4, Cullinet Integrated Dictionary; Chapter 5, IBM DB/DC Data Dictionary; Chapter 6, DATAMANAGER; Chapter 7, A Simple Dictionary Implementation; Chapter 8, Existing Problems and Solutions; and Chapter 10, Extensions.

The objective of this task is to identify dictionary entities, their interrelationships, and their attributes. Dictionary entities are the things about which data, metadata really, will be stored. A simple entity relationship diagram, such as Figure 7.1, is a good way to document the entities and their relationships.

Make sure that this diagram is accompanied by a good definition of each entity. It is very easy to go astray here. You'll be surprised how many different ideas there can be about the meaning of a word like system. Make sure that everyone who is involved in the project can agree on the acceptability of each definition. Also note that if everyone does not enter this activity with a spirit of cooperation and compromise, you may wrangle forever. It is not possible to achieve the one perfect set of dictionary entity definitions. It is essential to *negotiate* a set that everyone can live with. It is also essential to be certain that everyone has the same understanding of each. You should include an estimate of the number of occurrences of each entity to be documented in the dictionary.

It is important to make sure that each relationship is also documented and agreed upon. Try to include only those relationships that will be used. You can identify many relationships that you will never make use of. Maintaining these later will either be wasted effort or an impossibility. For each relationship, you should document the entities involved, the number of each entity type involved, and the reason for including it. The numeric estimate should include the minimum, maximum, and average number of entity occurrences for each type of relationship.

Finally, you should list and define the data items or elements that describe each entity type and relationship type. For each data item, you should have a good definition and a physical description.

Does all this sound familiar? It should. It represents the sort of data dictionary that is needed for any system design project. Very likely you will eventually store this *metadictionary* data in your dictionary. Let's hope thinking about this doesn't give you a headache!

Several points are important in this step. Be sure to think about how you will obtain the data and how you will use it. Including information that will never be used is pointless. It is likely that no one will want to maintain it. Be sure you have a way to capture the data. There is no point in providing a slot for data that cannot be maintained. *Including data that either cannot or will not be maintained will ultimately destroy the credibility of the dictionary.*

In other words, this step really complements the next step, Draft of Procedures. You can't complete one without the other. Our suggestion is to make a draft of the diagram and its supporting documentation, keeping notes about procedures as you go. Then address procedures. As you outline the procedures, keep notes regarding the use and capture of each piece of data. Then finalize both.

We'd better address the form of documentation. The diagram has been discussed above. The remainder should follow the form dictated by your standard methodology. Lacking a methodology, you should, as we noted before, refer to a text on system development.

Finally, note that at this point you should be addressing the needs of your organization, not the features of a particular dictionary. It is unrealistic to think you will be doing this in a vacuum. You will probably have some dictionary or some set of features in mind, but it is important to do the best you can at defining your needs, rather than searching for ways to use the features of a particular software package.

11.3.7   Draft of Procedures

This activity involves the identification of procedures that will be needed. A brief statement of the purpose, general nature, and contents of each will suffice for now. The actual procedure description will be written later.

The data dictionary we've started to design is really a data base. We can't separate its content from its intended uses. Another way of stating this is that the organization and the procedures that will be followed provide a context which makes the data and the database design meaningful. Additionally, we've noted repetitively that it is pointless to design a data base which contains data that will not be used or cannot be maintained. Let's address uses first and capture second. Then we'll look at standards and naming again.

Uses of Data. This is the place where we begin to address some difficult issues. So far, we've collected a lot of information, established some objectives, and documented some data we think we'd like to collect. Now it is time to ask how we will use the data to achieve the objectives. Presumably, we are going to all this trouble because the data will be used by specific people for specific purposes.

In section 7.2, Objectives, we stated a desire to document which programs, jobs, and systems access and update which data elements in which files and data base. Now we must ask why we are doing this and how the documentation will be used. The specifics of the answer will, of course, depend on your particular situation. But, let's take a shot at it.

This cross-reference will be used to assess the impact of any data change. That means it must be possible to find anything affected by a change to an element or type of element or record or file. Several things follow from this.

It must be possible for the intended user to gain access to a report which contains the desired information. The availability of an on-line inquiry is a very workable alternative. Lacking on-line inquiry, it would be wise to provide for special on-request reports that contain data about specific elements or types of elements. A complete listing of the content of the dictionary for a large operation could run to thousands of pages!

Appropriate keywords, classifications, and categories must be available to restrict the output from inquires and special report requests to manageable volumes and relevant data.

There must be procedures for requesting reports and distributing reports to the intended users and for distributing updated reports when changes render the existing reports obsolete.

The intended user must be aware that he or she has access to the data and must understand the content of the report or screen.

Some users will be sophisticated enough to prepare their own queries or report requests. Others will require assistance. Procedures for submitting requests and for obtaining assistance must be addressed.

Decisions must be made about who will be authorized to request or view which data and how authorizations will be requested and assigned.

Reviewing the information contained in the dictionary should become a step in the procedure for assessing the impact of any change. Note that change could be to the physical form of a particular data item or a class of data items. An example of the latter is a desire to change the year component of all dates from two digits to four digits. It might be a change in the way a particular item is computed or updated. It might be a change in the frequency of update or recalculation or the timing of the update or recalculation. Note also that applications or users affected by the change might be mainframe applications, Information Center applications, or even manual procedures.

Thus, it is necessary to ask a series of questions for each objective we've set.

Just how does the content of our dictionary contribute to the achievement of the objective?

Does the design facilitate extracting the needed information? Can you trace an access path for each retrieval?

Who will use the information?

How will they use it?

How will they obtain it?

Can output be restricted to manageable volumes?

Will recipients of the output understand it?

What existing procedures must be revised to ensure that this happens?

What new procedures must be created?

Which documents or manuals contain the procedures?

Who must approve any changes to a given procedure?

What must be done to make new procedures acceptable?

There are just too many possible variations of objectives and organizations to allow for comprehensive treatment of every possibility. The one example plus the guidelines will have to suffice.

Procedures for Maintenance. Appropriate maintenance procedures are equally important. They might seem more important, since data that cannot be obtained cannot be used. Do you think procedures for use are equally important or subsidiary? Why?

You should also keep in mind that the highly interrelated nature of dictionary data makes specific procedures for change very complex. We've looked at this in section 8.5, Again—What About Versions?

It is necessary to ask these questions for each piece of data incorporated in the design. You might also review section 7.5, Procedures, Sources of Data, and Uses of Data.

Can the data be obtained?

Can it be kept current?

Where is it available?

Who can provide it?

Who will provide it?

Can you be sure they will provide it and provide it in a timely manner? What will motivate them to do so?

In what form will they provide it?

Will it be necessary to devise paper forms for input? Is on-line input achievable? Generally, the latter is superior if hardware access is reliable and appropriate controls can be established.

When will they provide it?

What will the impact be on their existing practices and procedures?

How will dictionary maintenance be incorporated into existing procedures?

Which procedures must be revised?

Where and how are these procedures recorded?

Are new procedures required?

Who must approve the changes and new procedures?

How will dictionary input be audited? This issue is particularly important. Dictionary content will be only as good as the procedures for auditing and ensuring the update process.

Who will be responsible for the integrity of dictionary content?

Which checks and audits might be automated?

Will corrections be made in a timely manner?

Don't forget to plan for security of the dictionary data. Review section 8.8, Security Concerns.

Again, there are so many possible variations here that the best we can do is list the questions that need to be asked.

Active and Passive Dictionaries. The procedure for dictionary update cannot really be finalized until we know whether the dictionary will be active or passive (see section 3.8, Active Versus Passive)—but we haven't made a software selection yet.

We had better take a little time out to discuss this. First of all, as we noted in section 8.3.3, Software Selection, the specific product may already be a given for a variety of reasons, and that does not have to be bad. *Also, that does not alleviate the need for this logical design procedure we've been going through.*

Another important point here is that the difficulties you perceive in devising and implementing adequate procedures for use of a passive dictionary may become compelling arguments for the selection of a truly active dictionary. Bear in mind that the selection of a truly active data dictionary implies the selection and use of the companion DBMS and vice versa.

The final point is that this may not be as big an issue as it appears to be. A highly active dictionary is, of necessity, integrated with a particular data base management system. Few organizations can make a commitment to the use of one data base management system for everything. This is particularly true for a large organization or one that relies heavily on purchased packages. Thus, an active integrated dictionary, while it can be active for systems that utilize the related DBMS, will be passive for all systems that do not use the related DBMS. This means that most large organizations can have, at best, a dictionary implementation that is partly active and partly passive. This also raises the question of multiple dictionaries— which is our next topic.

How Many Dictionaries? This could have been discussed in section 11.3.6, A Logical Design for the Dictionary, but it is perhaps more appropriate here.

Multiple dictionaries are sometimes desirable, sometimes unavoidable. This is discussed in section 3.13, One More Complication: Packages and Tools Have Dictionaries, section 8.9, How Many Dictionaries?, section 10.6, Support Life Cycle Methodology, and section 10.7, Support Distributed Processing.

Several factors may motivate the move to multiple dictionaries.

We may have several different software products, each of which depends on its own integrated dictionary. These might be data base management systems or they might be purchased application packages.

We may have made a commitment to a specific DBMS, but have found that the associated dictionary just does not provide features that we consider essential.

We may need to be able to run several copies of a software package with an integrated dictionary on several different computers, or even on the same computer. In either case, each copy of the software is likely to require its own unique dictionary.

We may choose to separate dictionaries by function in order to maintain integrity of dictionary data. Separate dictionaries for test and production are one example. Separation by application area or subject data base is another.

We may choose to maintain separate dictionaries at different geographic locations. The motives and issues here would be the same as for any distributed system.

The need or desire for multiple dictionaries will affect our design and our procedures in a number of ways. First, it seems almost mandatory that we select one dictionary as the master or controlling dictionary. This means a physical dictionary occurrence as well as a product. The design of this dictionary will provide for a dictionary entity called DICTIONARY. This entity needs attributes, such as LOCATION, PURPOSE, or VENDOR. It needs to be related to entities representing the systems, programs, files, and other items documented within the dictionary it represents. It does not seem reasonable or possible to document all data elements and all details in the master dictionary.

Once again, the exact answers depend on your situation, but we can make some suggestions.

You should not put any more than is absolutely necessary in the master dictionary. It should provide a reference to the content of the other dictionaries. This should be in terms of the systems, files or databases, and general classes of data documented in each dictionary. (Classes of data means broad generic categories, such as customer data or accounting data.) It should contain data that must be interrelated or reported together.

Dictionaries that exist solely for the purpose of allowing a piece of software to function on a particular piece of hardware or in a particular software environment should contain the minimal information required for that purpose.

The criteria for duplicating identical metadata in multiple dictionaries are the need to cross-reference from one dictionary to another and the need to show information from several dictionaries on a single report or query.

Given the existence of multiple dictionaries, it becomes essential to implement procedures which ensure that metadata appearing in more than one dictionary is consistent and procedures which control the migration of metadata from one dictionary to another and ensure that it takes place in a timely and accurate manner. (Also see note 4 for chapter 10.) The migration from test to production status requires particular attention and must be integrated with procedures for the migration of systems from test to production.

A Comment on Procedures. In this book we place a lot of emphasis on procedures and controls. Unfortunately, most large enterprises maintain volume on volume of written procedures that are rarely referred to or followed. There are probably many reasons for this. Rather than attempt to explain this phenomenon, let's look at some characteristics of useful procedures.

Useful procedures are realistic. They do not ask people to do things that are impossible or can not be done in the time allotted.

Useful procedures have been developed in cooperation with the people who are expected to follow them.

Useful procedures are clearly and simply documented. They are easy to retrieve and interpret.

Useful procedure manuals are well organized and extensively indexed.

Useful procedures are written and organized in a manner which makes it possible to find the needed information quickly and easily.

Useful procedures are easy to remember because they reflect well thought out ways to accomplish specific tasks.

Procedures need to be sold. People must be convinced that there will be a benefit to the organization and to themselves.

People must be trained in the use of procedures. Most people are reluctant to search through volumes of information in order to find out what to do. There must be an ongoing effort to ensure that those who are expected to follow procedures are aware of the existence and content of the procedures.

Training must also be provided for new personnel and for those transferred from one function to another. Periodic refresher training and reinforcement is essential.

Management must demonstrate support for the procedures. Compliance must be monitored, audited, and made a part of performance evaluations.

Above all, procedures must be sensible and reasonable.

Naming Standards. As we discussed in section 8.4, What's in a Name?, naming standards are particularly important and particularly problematic. Based on that discussion, we offer the following approach. Review section 8.4 before you proceed.

Recognize the need for more than one type of name.

There is a need for an English-language name that will be meaningful to everyone, especially end users. Most dictionaries require the use of some comment or description area for this name. The format should be as free as possible. The notion of qualification should be used in constructing this name. Standard nomenclature should be employed whenever possible. It is necessary to defer to common usage; you cannot issue an edict that people must stop using one name and start using another.

Every dictionary entity needs at least one name that is constructed according to programming language rules.

There are likely to be as many of these as there are programming languages in use. Frequently the language rules dictate that these names must vary from language to language. Within a given program it is frequently necessary to have more than one unique name for multiple representations of the same data. These names could be arbitrary, but it is useful if they convey some reflection of the data represented. Qualification and prefixing are extremely useful here.

There is a great benefit in standardizing the names used as report headings and item identifiers on screens. These must be as descriptive as possible. They should be based on usage. A well-chosen name may eventually become the common name for the item.

Data element names are almost always the only big problem. Names for files, programs, and so on are usually much easier to standardize. Almost any orderly technique for assigning these is acceptable.

Our approach to naming is based on the observations cited above and is quite simple.

Most likely you already have standards for program names, file names, and the like. These probably consist of prefixes or suffixes that identify application areas combined with arbitrarily assigned numbers. Do not attempt to alter this standard unless you have an extremely good reason. If a change is necessary, look for the most concise and rational assignment you can find. Be sure to allow for the creation of new files, programs, and applications.

Develop a standard nomenclature for use in constructing qualified English-language names, such as "customer identifier for accounts receivable." Compile and document as much of the nomenclature as possible before the first name is assigned. Establish the rule that the basic purpose of the item comes first, followed by descriptors, followed by qualifiers. Here are a few more examples: "date of shipment for invoicing," "name of dependent for human resource records," and "date of birth of dependent.'' Once you've done the best you can with this, move on.

Establish standard prefixes or suffixes to identify specific systems, subsystems, and files or data bases. Keep these as short as possible. It is beneficial if they can relate to the existing standards for these entities.

Establish standard abbreviations for all words in the standard nomenclature. Create as many as possible before the first name is assigned. Keep them as short as possible. If you construct abbreviations on an as-needed basis, you are almost certain to end up with two or more abbreviations, a long and a short, for many words.

Standardize names consisting of a usage prefix followed by an abbreviation of the English-language name. Follow the rules of qualification, as discussed above. Do the best you can with this and move on.

It might be possible to revise names used in programs that have been written in house. We'll discuss this along with data conversion.

It is unrealistic to consider changing names used within purchased software. The possibilities for dealing with these are as follows. Employ some form of prefixing or suffixing in the dictionary. Keep the data about each package in a different dictionary. Use some form of classifying or indexing in conjunction with a versioning technique to identify the source of each name. Partition the dictionary using versioning or status. The first of these alternatives appears to be the best.

In evaluating naming remember that if there are two different fields in two different records, they are different things even if they do represent the same data. Each needs a unique name so that we can tell one from the other. At the same time, the names should indicate that these are in fact representations of the same data. Also, remember that we use qualified names all the time in our thinking; we just omit the qualifier whenever context makes our meaning clear. We speak of George, Gracie's husband George, George Burns, George Burns from California, or George Burns the comedian—whichever is appropriate at a given time. We also infer that a canary has characteristics common to all birds which have characteristics common to all mammals. We need to keep all of these points in mind when we think about names and naming standards.

11.4 ORGANIZATIONAL ISSUES

At this point you'll have to address the nature of the organization. As a matter of fact, this is intertwined with not only the logical design and the procedures, but also with the objectives. The nature of the organization dictates which goals are realistic and which are not. The existence of a procedure implies that a person situated at a particular place in the organization will perform it. The existence of a particular data item implies that some person at some location in the organization has followed some procedure to provide it. It also implies that there are specific people who will utilize it in specific ways—or at least this should be the case.

It is not at all clear that there is one single best way of organizing for management of a data dictionary or for data administration. Data Administration is an evolving discipline. Each organization must examine and evaluate itself and available techniques.

Let's list a few principles we need to be aware of here.

Given the existence of a shared data base that can be updated and used by many people scattered throughout an organization, there must be a central point of management and control; otherwise the situation will be chaotic and the data will be without value. A data dictionary is no exception to this rule.

Some of the work involved in implementing and operating a data dictionary is highly technical; some is not. In fact, some of the issues that must be addressed are highly political.

It does not make good sense for the individual charged with enforcing rules and procedures to be subordinate to those who must follow them.

No computer data base application will be successful in an organization that is not ready to accept it . Again, a data dictionary is no exception.

Data Administration is as much a function of business management as of data processing.

The ideal organization for successful implementation of a data dictionary will embody the elements shown in Figure 11.1. The existence of a data administration function will demonstrate a commitment to data resource management. It has been argued that an effective data administrator must report at a high level within the enterprise, preferably outside the data processing organization. This cannot be proven and may or may not be true. However, an effective data administrator must have good lines of communication with the end user community and must understand business functions and objectives. In addition, there must be solid evidence that corporate management recognizes the value of data resource management and supports the activities of the data administrator. He or she must also be in a position to communicate effectively with the data processing organization and obtain cooperation from system implementers. This latter issue is often neglected.

The existence of a separate data base administration function will serve as evidence of recognition that the technical management of the environment requires different skills and training than does the data administration function. The data base administrator may or may not report to the data administrator. It seems more important for the DBA to have good rapport and communication with the technical staff. The DBA must, without doubt, have good lines of communication with the DA. And, there must be a spirit of cooperation. The DBA must also have good lines of communication with system developers but must not be subservient to them. This function is often appropriately situated within a systems programming group.

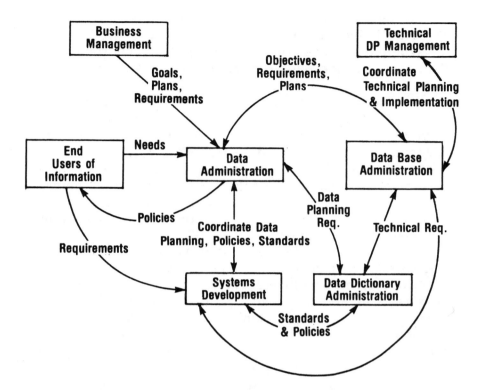

FIGURE 11.1   Elements of Data Resource Management

Effective data resource management requires communication and cooperation between the end user or business community and the data processing organization. Within the data processing organization, communication and cooperation between and among the highly technical groups and the system designers is essential.

The ideal organization provides for cooperation between a DA situated on the user side, a technical DBA, and a systems development organization. The spirit of cooperation is much more important than the specific organizational structure. Given management support and commitment, alternative structures should be effective. Given its absence, it is unlikely that any structure will succeed.

For more on this subject, you are referred to the literature on data administration and on management.

Where does the dictionary fit in? It is an important tool for data administrator, data base administrator, and system developer.

A data dictionary administrator should be responsible for the development and management of standards and procedures. Data dictionary administration also requires a combination of technical, analytical, and political skills.

If a mature data administration function exists, the data dictionary administrator should report to the data administrator. There should also be one individual or more within the DBA group who is responsible for technical implementation and maintenance issues.

If there is no data administration function, you should concentrate on a dictionary implementation that serves the needs of systems developers. The example given in Chapter 7 is more than ambitious enough. In this case, it would be realistic for the data dictionary administrator to report to the systems development manager. Everyone involved in the project should realize that when the data resource management function matures it will probably be reorganized. Here is a sample set of realistic objectives for a data dictionary administrator in this situation.

Document the data content and uses of new and existing systems.

Provide a basis for effective decision support and management information systems.

Educate data processing staff and end users regarding data concepts.

Lay the foundation for the evolution of an organization-wide data administration function.

Finally, remember that procedures can't be developed and implemented in a vacuum. They must be developed in light of the organizational structure.

11.5 SOFTWARE SELECTION

This is a good time to review the material on software selection in section 8.3. In that section we discussed the possibility that the dictionary software has already been selected, will be selected along with a DBMS, or will be selected for nontechnical reasons. In this section we will address the steps in a selection process. You should note that these steps are relevant to your dictionary project whether or not you have the luxury of making your own selection. There are several reasons for this.

You still need to determine the extent to which you will use the features of a particular data dictionary and how you will use them. It is necessary to identify the software features and facilities that you require in order to do this.

You may find that the "given" product just does not provide some essential feature or facility. In this case you have several choices. You can pretend the problem doesn't exist and start polishing your resume. You can determine which objectives in your plan must be altered. You can find a way to simulate the required facilities via extensibility or add-on software. You can give serious consideration to a multiple dictionary environment. We discussed the various motives for this in the subsection of 11.3, How Many Dictionaries.

This last option is probably the most workable technically. It may be very difficult to sell, however. Be prepared with a clear, simple explanation of the concept of multiple dictionaries. Be prepared with a comprehensive list of dictionaries and directories built into other software products that have been purchased or developed and the reasons why none of them will be suitable as your master dictionary.

Finally, you may have already determined that multiple dictionaries will be required.

With this in mind, let's review significant steps in the selection process.

11.5.1 Identify Software and Vendor Requirement

The first step is to identify software features required. You should review your objectives and your design, then prepare a list of required features. A listing of items you might consider important follows.

Presence of one or more specific dictionary entities or relationships.

Ability to create specific dictionary entities or relationships via extensibility.

Presence of extensibility features deemed necessary or useful.

Ability to represent data entities embodied in a particular DBMS, software package, or access method.

Requirement for an active or passive dictionary.

Dependence of a DBMS selected for purchase or already in house on a particular dictionary.

Dependence of the dictionary on a particular DBMS.

Existence or availability of data conversion aids.

Suitability to the operating environment in terms of memory requirements, operating system requirements, access method requirements, operator intervention requirements, and the like.

Suitability to the operating environment in terms of interface to an existing teleprocessing monitor. That is, what must be done to use the dictionary on line, and how easy or hard will this be?

Suitability to the operating environment in terms of interface to other software, such as source library systems and job scheduling systems. Ease of installation.

Presence of required input screens, inquiry screens, and reports.

Ease with which custom screens and reports can be generated.

Data independence. How will dictionary software changes affect a library of custom screens and reports?

'Friendliness'' of screens and reports.

Quality and availability of vendor documentation.

Quality and availability of vendor training.

Quality and availability of vendor support.

Presence in house of other products leased or purchased from the vendor of a dictionary.

Willingness of management to consider a particular vendor.

Once you've identified the features that you require, you should attempt to rank them according to importance and also to assign weights indicating the relative importance of each. You might use weights of three, two, and one for very important, important, and not very important.

11.5.2 Evaluation and Selection

Decision making is difficult. Decision making in the face of multiple criteria is particularly difficult. It is likely that no single dictionary package will excel in every category that you consider important.

You may be required by your management to follow a specific methodology or format. If so, this will probably imply or specify a technique for making a selection. Or, you may be schooled in or required to use a specific decision-making technique. If either of these is the case, you already know what to do next.

Otherwise, we suggest the following. Assign each product worthy of consideration a rating in each category. A scale of one to five would be appropriate. It is generally considered best to do this a category at a time, not a product at a time. That is, you prepare a matrix similar to Figure 11.2 and then assign ratings a row at a time. Next, multiply each rating by the weight assigned to that category and develop a score for each competing product. Theoretically, the product with the highest score wins.

Let's take some time out to reconsider this process. What have we really done? We've found a way to put a picture of a complex problem on one piece of paper so we can digest it. The mere fact of doing this should clarify the issues involved.

You may find that you don't really like the conclusion produced by this process. Then you should ask yourself if you are stubbornly clinging to a preconception or if there is a flaw in your process or ratings. You may note that you can, by changing the scale of ratings or of weights, or by changing a small number of ratings or weights, change the outcome. However, be aware that people often do this to justify the decisions which they want to make.

Understand that you are using a subjective process to quantify a complex problem. None of the weights or ratings are absolute. If they do, in fact, represent how you *and the rest of your organization* feel about each question, the result should be valid. It is difficult to make certain that this is the case. But, if for example, the consensus is that one specific decision variable is much more important than all others, it is reasonable to assign it a much higher weight. It is also reasonable to reject out of hand any product that does not possess an essential quality or feature. But, be certain that there is agreement that this is the case.

In most organizations, this software selection process involves a combination of technical and political issues. The technique described provides a convenient method for focusing

Criteria		Products			
	Wgt	A	B	C	D
1	3	5	3	1	4
2	3	3	4	5	1
3	2	4	4	4	5
4	2	5	3	2	3
5	1	2	2	2	5
6	1	2	3	5	4
Ranking		46	40	35	40

FIGURE 11.2   Decision Matrix Format

attention on the issues and viewing the problem from a reasonable perspective. Since this is not a treatise on decision making, we'll stop here and assume that a reasonable selection is made.

11.5.3   Could You Write Your Own Dictionary?

All dictionaries available today probably lack some feature or features that you will consider desirable. The better ones allow for circumvention of most of these shortcomings via extensibility and customized reporting. It is, however, tempting to consider the possibility of developing one's own dictionary. This is particularly true since the advent of a number of relatively easy-to-use relational data base management systems. However, developing a custom data dictionary in house is still not a realistic alternative for most organizations. We've already discussed this in the subsection of 8.3, Software Selection. Let's review some of the issues.

Designing and writing a data dictionary would be a major project. The use of an "easy to use" DBMS does not alter this fact.

Vendors of the leading products have a big investment in the design and coding of logic for maintaining and relating dictionary entities, entering maintenance, checking for errors, reporting maintenance and dictionary content, back up and recovery of dictionary data, interface to compilers, interface to source library systems, interface to operating systems, and on and on.

These vendors are committed to maintenance and support of their products in the face of new or revised hardware and software requirements.

They devote considerable effort to research and to enhancement of their products.

In most cases, there are active user groups that are a source of a lot of good ideas and information regarding the use of data dictionaries.

Suffice it to say that designing, developing, implementing, *and maintaining* a data dictionary is a significant project. Few organizations are prepared to make the necessary commitment. It seems doubtful that the benefits could outweigh the effort except in special situations.

11.6   DETAILED REPORT AND PLAN

Once again, it is appropriate to report findings and present a plan for the next phase. Several points are worth repeating.

If your organization has a standard methodology or format, you should follow it.

In formulating the plan, you will have the benefit of having read the remaining sections of this book.

Your plan and cost estimate will represent revisions to the original plan and estimate based on the findings of this phase of the study.

You should be sure to provide a brief, clear management summary.

11.6.1 Cost and Benefit Analysis

You should be able to support your recommendation and plan with a detailed discussion of problems, objectives, costs, and benefits. Once again you are referred to section 8.3.2, How to Justify a Dictionary, for a discussion of the benefit issue. The software costs should be known. The estimate should include operating costs and implementation costs. Implementation costs can best be developed via a detailed breakdown of the remaining tasks. Don't forget training for both the data dictionary administration staff and all users of the data dictionary. For more details on cost versus benefit analysis, you are again referred to any standard text on systems analysis and design.[6]

11.6.2 The Data Conversion Issue

In this report and plan you will have to come to grips with the data conversion issue. This is a big issue and a big problem. We have already discussed it some in section 8.3. Let's talk about it again.

Many papers and articles, as well as a lot of the vendor promotional material, tend to ignore or minimize this issue. In fact, it is often the biggest stumbling block to the successful implementation of a data dictionary. One possible approach would be to ignore the issue and hope it goes away. This is not entirely unrealistic. If there are major systems that are in the process of being replaced or are scheduled to be replaced soon, the best thing to do would be to pick up the needed definitions as part of the new projects.

The alternative, of course, is to research the needed data and place it in the data dictionary. The degree of difficulty you can expect here will depend on the quality of the methodology originally used in the development of each system, the quality of the methodology used for subsequent maintenance, the quality of existing documentation, and the existence or lack of consistently enforced naming standards. It is generally necessary to evaluate this on a system-by-system basis. Even organizations that now have the best methodologies and standards still have to contend with many old systems that were developed without the benefit of these tools.

In order to plan or evaluate the conversion, it is necessary to identify the source and consistency of every piece of metadata.

The actual conversion process can be facilitated by software designed to scan existing programs and job control statements and develop appropriate data dictionary maintenance transactions. Two examples of this are Cullinet's Dictionary Loader[7] and Data Dictionary Composer.[8] The Dictionary Loader is uniquely designed for use with Cullinet's Integrated Data Dictionary. The Composer is of a more general nature. You might consider writing your own conversion system, but remember that this could turn out to be a lot more work than it is worth.

A software-assisted conversion can eliminate a lot of manual drudgery—the thing that computers do best. It is unlikely, however, that you can achieve a successful conversion without considerable manual intervention. It is still necessary to review and possibly modify all metadata extracted by software before placing it in the dictionary. The extent of modification will be directly proportional to the extent of standardization of names.

It is necessary to identify all names used for any given dictionary entity and also all dictionary entities that are representations of the same real world entity. You might want to review the naming standards section in this Chapter and section 8.4, What's In A Name, once more if this sounds confusing, It is also essential to identify any situations where the same name stands for two different dictionary entities or real-world entities. This could be the more insidious problem, by far.

Given multiple names for the same entity, they must either be changed or dealt with as synonyms and aliases. Given one name for multiple entities, they must either be changed or dealt with through versioning or multiple dictionaries. As you might expect, data elements and their names present the most problems. This can be compounded by a need to have more than one unique name for the same piece of data due to the constraints of programming languages and techniques.

Once the problems are identified, some one must decide what to do about them. Then it must be done. By now you should realize that coming up with a unique name to be stored in the dictionary is not enough. It is necessary to change it in the original source or create a reference to the original source as well. Changing the original source could involve extensive changes to existing programs, job control statements, *and documentation*. This is not something to be undertaken lightly-and it is a very labor-intensive activity.

Data Dictionary Composer, for example, will identify most if not all occurrences of these problems. It will also make many of the necessary alterations to the dictionary maintenance transactions and to existing programs and job control statements. It can also be instructed to place prefixes on groups of names. However, someone must review each individual problem, decide how to resolve it, and prepare the transactions that will instruct Data Dictionary Composer regarding the desired resolution. This will usually require knowledge of the application and of the business use of the data.

Conversion software cannot automatically generate definitions for data entities. There will be data relationships that cannot be identified automatically. And, of course, manual intervention will be required if existing documentation is to be corrected.

This is not intended as a statement that conversion software has no value. It should however convince you that this can be a big job even if it is partially automated. A typical large organization could expect the conversion process to take three to five years at best. It is important to realize this, plan for it, and decide which systems and applications should be worked on first. Application of the 80/20 rule is very appropriate here. Twenty percent of the effort might reap eighty percent of the benefit. It is possible that some systems may never be completely documented in the dictionary. It would be very reasonable to rank the existing systems according to perceived difficulty of conversion and also according to the perceived need for incorporating them in the dictionary. Then a conversion plan could be developed on the basis of need and also on the basis of ease of conversion. As we've already noted, systems scheduled for early retirement might best be ignored.

Figure 11.3 illustrates the basic conversion process. It is based on Composer Technology Corporation and Cullinet documentation.

The really important points from this section are worth repeating.

Dealing with new development is much easier than dealing with systems that already exist.

However, you can't plan a data dictionary or data resource management project without taking existing systems into consideration.

Your plan should be based on careful evaluation of your objectives and the nature of each individual system.

Software can be used to automate part of the process, but capture of metadata about existing systems is very labor-intensive and time-consuming.

Realistic goals and careful planning are essential.

11.7 IMPLEMENTATION

We are going to discuss actual implementation in less detail for several reasons. Some things are highly dependent on the specific software you select. These will be covered in the vendor's technical manuals and training program. Some things

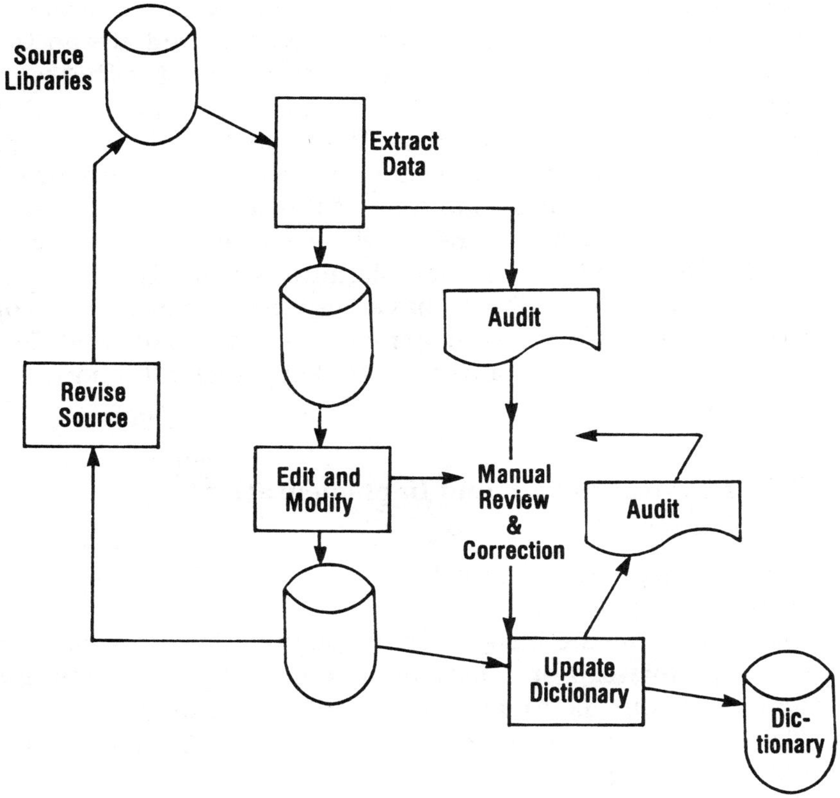

FIGURE 11.3   Conversion Process

are highly dependent on your specific environment. If you have done all the planning that has been recommended, implementation will be relatively easy. *This does not mean that a failure to follow through here cannot nullify all the work that has been done so far.*

11.7.1   Vendor Training

A lot of time should have been spent preparing for the implementation phase. A lot of money will have been spent on the software. It just doesn't make sense to try to compromise on training. Everyone who will be involved should attend the appropriate vendor-conducted training. Frequently the sales person will have emphasized the quality of the software and minimized the need for training. Don't be fooled. It is very important that the actual implementation be firmly supported by a comprehensive understanding of the software.

Data processing literature is full of stories about projects that failed because the front-end planning was not done or was not done thoroughly. There have also been many cases of failure caused by technical incompetence at the back end. For some reason, these are not as well publicized. Don't ignore the importance of either.

11.7.2   Physical Design and Implementation

This phase involves utilizing the features of the software to implement the logical design.

Depending on the complexity of your design, this may be very straightforward or it may involve considerable ingenuity in the use of your dictionary's extensibility features.

This is a good time to review section 8.7, Technical and Operational Issues.

Here is a list of important steps.

Translate the logical design into a physical design. Follow the vendor's instructions on this.

Prepare the necessary control statements to define the configuration to the software. Follow the vendor's instructions on this.

Calculate disk space requirements for a test case. Follow the vendor's instructions on this. Don't neglect journal, back-up, and report files. If you plan multiple dictionaries, you may also need space for files of data reflecting transfer of information from one dictionary to another.

Write any custom reports using the dictionary's reporting facility. Remember, the reports that have been provided were probably written by technicians for technicians. They may require modification to make them suitable for the uses you plan. Each standard report should be reviewed with the users of the dictionary. Problems may not come to light until the actual testing. Allow time for this in your planning.

Generate any special screens. All the comments about reports also apply here.

Determine what changes, if any, must be made to existing software, such as the teleprocessing monitor, security software, and the job control scheduling systems.

Develop test data. There are two criteria for test data. On the technical side, it should be carefully planned to test all features of the implementation. In addition, the same test data, if well thought out, can be used for training and experimentation involving the end users of the dictionary.

Prepare the necessary job control statements.

Implement the test version.

Test. This is a step you might tend to neglect. Don't.

Remember, you have selected a specific set of options from the many provided by a complex software product. You may have erred in your design. You may have erred in your specification of control statements. There could be errors in the vendor-supplied software. You may have selected some combination of options that was never chosen before. Careful testing of the software and your procedures is essential. Be sure to verify the accuracy of your space calculations.

If you plan to implement multiple dictionaries, be sure to test your migration procedures and your procedures for ensuring consistency and integrity.

Be sure to check out the interface to any teleprocessing monitor and any changes which may be required to the teleprocessing monitor.

Don't forget to test your security procedures.

Be sure to test your proposed operating procedures and validate these with the operations staff. It is important that they look on the actual dictionary as production work and not something the programmers run. This is also the time to firm up your thinking on report generation and distribution.

Calculate the space requirement for your production dictionary. Be sure to allow for growth. Enlarging a dictionary later may be very difficult.

Prepare job control statements for the production dictionary.

Be sure to do some testing with the production version as well before you commit real data to it.

11.7.4   Standards and Procedures

This step should consist of formalizing and publishing the standards and procedures that have been developed and identified in previous steps. Note that some procedures and standards will be contained in a data dictionary procedures manual, but others will be incorporated in other documents such as a system development methodology or a programming standards manual. The following is primarily a checklist.

Standards.   Relevant standards include:

Naming standards

Standard keywords and abbreviations

Standards for writing definitions

Incorporation of dictionary maintenance into system development methodology

Maintenance of source libraries

Procedures. Relevant procedures include:

Submission and processing of dictionary maintenance

Deletion of data that is no longer required

Control of back-up files, dictionary restoration, dictionary reorganization

Monitoring space utilization

Control of statuses and versions

Submission and processing of report requests

Audit and correction of dictionary content

Migration of data from dictionary to dictionary and from test status to production

Verification of consistency between dictionaries, source libraries, and other repositories of *metadata*

Monitoring of changes to the operating environment

Don't neglect the design of appropriate input forms and checklists.

Note that procedures for adding, modifying, or deleting data often must specify a particular sequence of operations. The vendor's documentation will discuss this.

Operating Guides. These must be in accord with practices established at your installation.

11.8   TRAINING and PUBLICITY

This is another critical step. It is essential that *everyone* who must provide data, use data, or in any way be affected by the dictionary understand what is expected, what will be provided, and why it is important. This is an activity that goes on forever. There will always be new personnel to train and advise. There will be enhancements to the dictionary and the dictionary environment. Previous training will need reinforcement.

11.9   MAINTENANCE

There will be new releases of the dictionary software. There will be problem fixes from the vendor. There will be problems to diagnose and resolve. Some changes will be necessitated by changes to other software. This maintenance of dictionary software is an ongoing activity. Staffing level depends on the complexity of your environment. You should at minimum be sure that someone is responsible and that there is adequate backup.

11.10   ENHANCEMENT

Enhancements and changes should be treated just like changes to any other business system. The dictionary contains data that is vital to the operation of the business. It should not be modified in a haphazard manner.

11.11   POST MORTEM—AND WHAT'S NEXT?

It is an excellent idea to schedule a post-implementation review. This should occur after implementation is complete and data conversion is well under way. All facets of the implementation should be reviewed to determine what problems exist, which of them must be corrected, and how to do it.

11.12 PHEW!

The final chapter consists of a few remarks on things omitted and some suggestions for the future.

NOTES

1. William R. Durrell, *Data Administration: A Practical Guide to Successful Data Management* (New York: McGraw-Hill, 1985).

2. Ronald G. Ross, *Data Dictionaries and Data Administration: Concepts and Practices for Data Resources Management* (New York: ANACOM, 1981).

3. James A. Senn, *Analysis and Design of Information Systems* (New York: McGraw-Hill, 1984).

4. Dennis G. Severance, Tutorial on Senior Management Control of Computer Based Systems conducted at the IEEE Trends and Applications Conference held in Gaithersburg, MD May 23–24, 1984.

5. G. B. Davis, "Strategies for Information Requirements Determination," *IBM Systems Journal* 21 (1982) pp. 4–30.

6. See especially Senn, op cit.

7. For more information, see *Dictionary Loader User's Guide* (Westwood, Mass.: Cullinet Database Systems, 1982).

8. For more information, see *Data Dictionary Composer Reference Manual* (Santa Clara, Calif.: Composer Technology Corporation, 1985). This manual can be obtained from the corporation at 3062 Millar Street, Santa Clara CA 95051.

12 Parting Comments

Two more questions that you might ask come to mind. One is, "Do you really expect anyone to do all that planning? The answer is, "Possibly not, but you'd be a lot better off if you did." As we've noted, many data dictionary projects just sort of happened. Someone may have purchased a DBMS with an integrated dictionary such as IDMS, or someone may have been convinced that a dictionary such as the IBM DB/DC Data Dictionary would be a valuable adjunct to a DBMS. Once a data dictionary has been started without adequate forethought it is likely that either it will grow in a very haphazard manner or it will never approach its true potential. Frequently the impact, the amount of effort required, and the political ramifications will have been grossly underestimated.

Here are the final words on this. The planning steps outlined in Chapter 11 are not that onerous. They are workable. The result will be a much sounder implementation. The more of this you do and the more you prepare ahead of time for problems, the better off you will be. It could well make the difference between success and failure.

Here's the other question you might ask. "What do I do if I'm already in a mess that was caused by lack of planning and foresight?" Clearly, the answer depends on the degree of mess and the specific problems. The most workable approach would be to review Chapter 11 and try to determine where you went astray. It will be necessary for you to evaluate your specific situation. However, if you never made your conceptual dictionary model, you'd best develop two models now. One will be for the dictionary you have. The other will be for the dictionary you'd like to have. Identify as many specific problems as you can. Determine what procedures and standards you have and what changes or additions are needed. Then map out a migration plan. It might be feasible to make a few enhancements. It might be necessary to start over. This can't be determined without the facts of a specific situation.

Finally, the author would like to believe that no matter what your present situation, this book has contributed to a better understanding that will lead to a better environment in your data processing situation.

Index